Innovations in Education Series
Edited by Robert J. Brown

1. Edward J. Dirkswager, ed. *Teachers as Owners: A Key to Revitalizing Public Education.* 2002.
2. Darlene Leiding. *The Won't Learners: An Answer to Their Cry.* 2002.

THE WON'T LEARNERS

An Answer to Their Cry

Innovations in Education Series, No. 2

Darlene Leiding

A SCARECROWEDUCATION BOOK

The Scarecrow Press, Inc.
Lanham, Maryland, and Oxford
2002

A SCARECROWEDUCATION BOOK

Published in the United States of America
by Scarecrow Press, Inc.
A Member of the Rowman & Littlefield Publishing Group
4720 Boston Way, Lanham, Maryland 20706
www.scarecroweducation.com

PO Box 317
Oxford
Ox2 9RU, UK

British Library Cataloguing in Publication Information Available

Library of Congress Cataloging-in-Publication Data

Leiding, Darlene, 1943–
    The won't learners : an answer to their cry / Darlene Leiding.
        p. cm.—(Innovations in education ; no. 2)
    "A ScarecrowEducation book."
    Includes bibliographical references.
    ISBN 0-8108-4317-X (alk. paper)—ISBN 0-8108-4302-1 (pbk. : alk. paper)
        1. Underachievers—United States. 2. Dropouts—United States—Prevention. 3.
    Educational change—United States. I. Title. II. Innovations in education
    (Lanham, Md.) ; no. 2.

LC4691 .L45 2002
371.93—dc21
                                                                    2002021204

⊗™ The paper used in this publication meets the minimum requirements of
American National Standard for Information Sciences—Permanence of Paper for
Printed Library Materials, ANSI/NISO Z39.48-1992.
Manufactured in the United States of America.

CONTENTS

ACKNOWLEDGMENTS

One person cannot accomplish anything alone. We are all intercon-
nected and it takes many to make anything a reality. This book is no
exception.

Credit must go first to Dr. Robert Brown, educational leadership professor at the University of St. Thomas and my friend. Bob put up with
me, encouraged me, offered invaluable advice, and shared his wisdom
and expertise before and during the entire process. He challenged me
to strive for professional excellence.

I offer thanks to the parents, students, and staff who shared their
ideas, questions, and concerns with me. Their visions became the foundation of the school that I created. I hope this book is of value to them
and to others committed to sharing their lives with our won't learners.

Others contributed as well. I am grateful to Joe Nathan, director of
the Center for School Change at the University of Minnesota, and to
Nancy Smith, former director of the New Twin City Charter School
Movement. Both generously shared their insights and expertise. Their
encouragement and friendship helped me with my writing.

Special thanks to Bruce Turnbaugh, my lead teacher, who provided
critical advice and assistance. His thirty-five years of teaching expertise,
patience, and humor helped make this endeavor an enjoyable task.

Two close friends have inspired and encouraged me. Both are in education and have been part of my life for over thirty years. Judy Schulze, early childhood educator and Christian youth director, lives down the block; Jane Deeming, educator and philosopher, lives across the country in Los Angeles. Both have devoted their lives to educating our won't learners.

I wish to thank Tom Koerner and Scarecrow Publishing for giving me the chance to share my passion for education and tips for success in the form of this book.

Finally, this book would not have been possible without the support and encouragement of the two most important people in my life: my husband, Marty, and my daughter, Wendy. Marty is my partner, my friend, my confidant, and the one constant in my life. Marty has given me more than thirty-five years of advice, challenge, and support. He has shared my visions and dreams. Wendy is an inspiration because of her youth, vibrancy, and trust in the educational system. Their love and support fill my life and provide me with the motivation and capacity to reach for my dreams.

FOREWORD

The American Education system is touted as being one of the best in the world. For many people, it is. However, for approximately one million students each year, it is untenable. They drop out of school. Others stay in school, but perform well below their ability level and become "in-school" dropouts. What happens to these "out-of-school" dropouts? Where do they go? What do they do? What are the economic and social costs of all of these dropouts? In a nation that was founded on liberty and justice for all, is the deprivation of opportunity that faces these students acceptable to us?

Do we even care?

Thankfully, the answer is yes.

The rapid rise in the number of alternative schools, professional organizations, and even the launching of the new *Alternative Network Journal* are proof of this. They are proof that "tinkering with the system" (a phrase coined by Tyack and Cuban) works.

In this book, Dr. Leiding aptly identifies these students as "won't learners," as opposed to "can't learners." The most important thing that she stresses is that these students do have enormous talents, ingenuity, energy, and creativity. They have everything it takes to make it.

At the same time, these students face incredible barriers to learning. The "won't learners" demonstrate poor attendance, are often tardy to class, cause disturbances and disruptions, are suspended and even expelled.

They fail to accumulate enough credits to move on to the next grade, and drop out in large numbers as soon as they become of age. They are young people from troubled families, young people who are angry and alienated, young people who are bright and bored, and, most of all, are young people who feel lost or frustrated in large schools.

"Won't learners" are in very poor educational shape, a situation caused mostly by problems they brought with them to the kindergarten door, particularly poverty, physical and emotional handicaps, lack of health care, difficult family conditions, and violent neighborhoods.

But acknowledging enormous problems *outside* schools does not mean that education cannot do a much better job at helping strengthen youngsters *inside* schools.

I *can* imagine classrooms where "won't learners" are enthusiastic and absorbed in activities, because this is my area of expertise. Students take time to talk with peers, ask advice, and admire each other's work. Projects are interdisciplinary, with many opportunities for hands-on learning. The work is challenging, related to real life, and is rich with meaning. Central themes are designed to challenge students at their own levels and appeal to a wide variety of interests.

For those educators unfamiliar to alternative schools, this scenario might be difficult to imagine. And for those people, we have this book.

The Won't Learners is a book about parents, teachers, community members, and students coming together to make a difference. A very interesting part of chapter 4 is a list of things that parents want from their child's school. Usually, the school tells the parents what it wants from them!

In the words of Lyndon B. Johnson, "Every child must be encouraged to get as much education as he has the ability to take. We want this not only for his sake—but for the nation's sake. Nothing matters more to the future of our country: not military preparedness—for armed might is worthless if we lack the brain power to build a world of peace; not our productive economy—for we cannot sustain growth without trained manpower; not our democratic system of government—for freedom is fragile if citizens are ignorant."

Dr. Carole Mottaz, Coordinator
Renaissance Academy in River Falls, Wisconsin
    Author, *Breaking the Cycle of Failure: How to Build and Maintain Quality Alternative Schools*

INTRODUCTION

One can resist the invasion of armies, but not the invasion of ideas.

—Victor Hugo

The Violent Generation, the Hollywood Generation, the Ambitious Generation, the Scapegoat Generation, Generation X, Generation Y, the "Won't Learners" Generation. From sociologists and journalists to parents and educators, adults categorize today's teenagers with a slew of conflicting labels. But what do we really know about this group of twelve- to eighteen-year-olds, a population of more than 30 million people? Can we adequately generalize about today's youth culture in a way that makes sense, not just to those who label teens but also to teens themselves?

Part of the difficulty involves the ambivalent images of today's youth. Some see that teenagers are outperforming their teachers and parents in technology; others worry that they are secretive, unsupervised, and just a Web site or a video game away from becoming dangerous or violent. Some agree that the media exploit teens through advertising and television whereas others feel that today's teens, the savvy children of baby boomers, actually control an increasingly teen-driven market.

Generation X, that rebellious population characterized by shopping malls, cynicism, and the 1970s television reruns, has finally given way to the next generation, raised more on the Internet and video games than on *The Brady Bunch* and the "Fonz." Who are they? How are they represented? And what, if any, common experiences do they share and bring into the schools?

We do not need to revisit press coverage of the late 1990s school shootings to hear why teens are in trouble. Although generation gaps have always existed, and older generations have always disparaged the activities and interests of the young, the way we talk about teens has shifted. No longer symptomatic of society's ills, the youth are seen as the root cause, at least in the minds of adults who fear and misunderstand them.

Henry Geroux, author of *Channel Surfing*, says, "Youth are no longer seen as at risk, they are the risk." The Public Agenda's (1999) report, *Kids These Days, 99: What Americans Really Think about the Next Generation*, underscores that fear. According to the report, more than seven in ten adults think that teens are "rude," "irresponsible," or "wild." Moreover, adults say that teens lack values, character, and basic civility. This is reality, despite the fact that the majority of teens surveyed felt that they have good relationships with their parents, strong religious beliefs, and good friends.

The educational media also portray a new deterioration of teen values. One lead article in *The American School Board Journal* is titled "A Generation of Cheaters" (Bushweller 1999). The lead article presents results from a 1998 survey of 356 high school teachers, stating that nine out of ten teachers believe that cheating is a problem, and half state that they encounter student cheating in most of their classes. According to teachers, this is because of an "erosion of ethics in a self-centered culture."

Others argue that these negative assertions simply do not measure up. Statistics show that juvenile crime has fallen, teen pregnancy has dropped, and teen drug use has declined. Mike Males, author of *The Scapegoat Generation* (1996), attacks these myths head on. Youth are less violent, they take better care of themselves, they are less self-destructive, and they take fewer drugs than in past decades. Unfortunately, he says, we focus on the sensational aspects of teen's lives, such as abnormal occurrences of violence.

What may add to this disturbing representation of youth are the negative media portrayals, which show teens as uninterested in the world around them, materialistic, and anti-intellectual. Particularly offensive are stereotypes of young African American males, who are often depicted as hostile, criminal, violent, or valued only for their athletic ability.

At the same time, youth culture is everywhere in the media. Teens seem to be running the show, or at least running Hollywood, as the *New York Times Magazine* (1999) suggests in a cover story, "Teensel Town"— thus, the overwhelming number of teen movies and television shows, from *Drive Me Crazy* to *Dawson's Creek*.

Henry Geroux argues that for youth culture to thrive, it must find a medium that allows self-representation and an authentic exploration of youth values and concerns. Instead of offering teens self-expression, the media (and ultimately those who own the media) control what is aired. In addition, they create shows that are generally not about real teenage lives, but are adult fantasies of what teens' lives might be like.

Enter into this picture the "won't learners." They are the students who fail to succeed in traditional elementary, middle, and high schools. The won't learners include large numbers of dropouts who would not or could not stay, alleged "pushouts" encouraged by school personnel not to remain. The won't learners also include students who have graduated despite evidence that they remain functionally illiterate. Charges abound with respect to our system's failure to meet the needs of the noncollege-bound students, "the forgotten half" as currently dubbed.

The won't learners demonstrate poor attendance, are often tardy to class, cause disturbances and disruptions, are suspended and even expelled. Won't learners fail to accumulate enough credits to move on to the next grade, and drop out in large numbers as soon as they become of age. Won't learners are young people from troubled families, young people who are angry and alienated, young people who are bright and bored, and most of all, are young people who feel lost or frustrated in large schools. They are at risk for dropping out or have already dropped out.

Won't learners need to be identified and dealt with in different ways.

A won't learner can be an *avoider of responsibility*. This learner may be friendly and easygoing, but avoids responsibilities and is forgetful, distracted, or unmotivated. This learner can be helped by setting realistic expectations for achievement and by stressing the connection between effort and outcome.

A won't learner can be a *worrier*. Are these learners perfectionists or procrastinators? Assisting each learner to understand his or her abilities can be an answer for a worrier.

Some won't learners are *seekers/philosophers*. This introspective child may be emotional, philosophical, and searching for identity. Teachers and parents need to be good listeners to help them achieve.

A won't learner can be a *misbehaver*. Children whose creative needs are not met may misbehave and underachieve to define themselves as separate people. Can we show them more appropriate ways to satisfy needs?

Finally, a won't learner may be a *victim of discrimination*. Children who refuse to learn because of discrimination, for whatever reason, need to have those experiences and feelings acknowledged. A safe environment needs to be established for this learner, and high-achieving role models and friends need to be identified.

Won't learners are in very poor educational shape, a situation caused mostly by problems they brought with them to the kindergarten door, particularly poverty, physical and emotional handicaps, lack of health care, difficult family conditions, and violent neighborhoods. We must target our resources and focus our concern on improving the system by working on the students who are at highest risk of school failure.

The won't learners are building their own revolution. The won't learners rebel against a traditional curriculum of mathematics, science, reading, and writing. They are getting conflicting messages of how to model behavior. The home and family should be the responsible party but often are not, and it falls upon the schools to pick up the slack. Teachers should guide the process. Kids are educating themselves in many cases, and they feel disconnected because school is no longer central in their lives. Personalities and identities are in constant flux.

When you teach won't learners in public schools, especially in the inner city, you by and large are dealing with young people for whom learning and academic achievement is not even close to being a priority. They are growing up in an environment devoid of literature or college-educated men and women. Many have already given up on school, or they read and write so badly that they understand little of what goes on in school (and consequently hate it, are bored, cause trouble, dropout, etc.). There are always the exceptions, but we are still told to teach to the average student in the class. Even in the rare chance that administrators and parents give teachers the support and tools to actually teach, many instructors are going to have a hard time, the test scores will be low, and the students will be violent, bored, or discontented.

The question that we face is, "What can educators do to reconnect with today's youth?" The gap in academic achievement between the won't learners (White, Asian, American Indian, Hispanic, and African American) is an enigmatic problem. It is often referred to as an intractable problem. Why, for all our efforts since the early 1960s, have we been unable to close this gap? Too often, the educational system gets caught up in protecting its own interests and forgets why it exists: to give *all* learners a high-quality education.

Is it reasonable to ask a school to be able to serve *all* of the students equally well? Can schools be effective in helping the many high academic achievers who plan to attend our best colleges and universities? If they focus on that population, the answer should be yes. But what about when they also serve a sizeable portion of at-risk students who are likely to drop out and who won't learn, and the whole spectrum of abilities that falls in between these extremes? Is it fair and reasonable to expect that a single, common approach will be able to educate a diverse population to be successful in achieving such a goal? If scarce resources or other factors make it difficult to adequately fund multiple pedagogical approaches tailored to best fit student needs, some are bound to be less well served. Diversity in the student population extends beyond academic ability to include interests, knowledge, goals, and aspirations for careers and lifestyles. A one-size-fits-all approach will not fit very many students.

Educators, parents, community leaders, and policymakers all agree that significant problems in our society are producing troubled families and challenging our youth. It is vital to work toward a more just and fair society that will prize all youth and strengthen all families.

If competence is achieved, other problems begin to recede. A recent PBS documentary featured a psychiatrist who said of a girl who had problems in junior high that until she learns to deal with her feelings, she is not going to have academic success. To hell with her feelings! She will be a transformed person the minute she has competencies and skills that she knows are marketable in the real world and she is given a prognosis for a future, for a happy life. This is what schools can do for students.

We—teachers, administrators, and staff members, as well as parents and community members—need to define the problem for what it really is rather than go through a calculus of racial identity. We all need to be more courageous, and we need to understand that we will be stigmatized for speaking frankly on these issues. In the long run, it is like jumping into cold water: after a minute, the shock is over with and you simply get used to it.

Rather than dealing with what we can do with our won't learners to help them become whatever they want to be now and in the future, we have spent our time and resources on analyzing the past. The won't learners have enormous talents, ingenuity, energy, and creativity. They have everything it takes to make it. We simply must help them tap into the resources that make it happen.

One question we face is, "What can educators do to reconnect with today's youth?" We can start by closing the gap between what the school curriculum offers and what the students are educating themselves for. We must find ways to bring new attention and energy to the won't learn-ers without losing our focus on all learners.

We are mistaken if we believe that discipline, dropouts, and drugs are what are wrong with today's schools. Serious as these are, they are symp-toms of a much larger underlying problem, which is that far too many capable students make little or no effort to learn. These students have been described earlier as the won't learners.

> "Am I understanding this? Have I learned anything? If I don't learn anything, then I've wasted my time."
>
> —Tenth-grade boy, a won't learner

This problem is not new. Criticism of the schools for low student achievement and recommendations to improve them have been offered more or less continuously since the end of World War II. Many students, at least 50 percent by eighth grade who are intelligent enough to do well, many even brilliantly, do poorly. Many of these students do not even finish the tenth grade. Most do not learn enough to become profi-cient in the basic skills at a sixth grade level. A significant group does not even learn to read; all appear to hate school.

To deal with students who are not working in school, we could continue to talk endlessly about improving the curriculum—but we have been doing that since *Sputnik* with no noticeable effect. We are all aware that this talk has not significantly reduced the number of students who do not choose to apply themselves in school. We need to stop talking in generalities and begin to talk about some specific changes in the structure of our teaching and in the role of the teacher in that new structure. If we do not advocate for change, we will not make a dent in the growing number of unmotivated students who are essentially forced to attend school. Many students come to school for lack of something better to do, but most of these students drop out well before graduation.

Because we seem unable to get more than half of the students involved in working hard in almost all public schools, we may have gone as far as we can go with the traditional structure of our schools. This structure, with which we are all familiar, is a teacher in the front of the classroom facing thirty to forty students sitting in rows. Traditionally, the teacher is the educational leader; all that goes on in that classroom depends on him or her. Each student learns as an individual depending only on himself/herself and what he/she can get from a busy teacher. Students do not depend on each other, are in competition for grades, and have little motivation to help each other. The less their classmates learn, the better it is for them.

Imagine, if you will, classrooms where students (the won't learners) are enthusiastic and absorbed in activities. Yet they take time to talk with peers, ask advice, and admire each other's work. Projects are interdisciplinary and the students have many opportunities for hands-on learning. The work is challenging, related to real life, and rich with meaning. Central themes are designed to challenge students at their own levels and appeal to a wide variety of interests. This scenario personifies many alternative schools today. These schools are answering the cry of the won't learners. The focus of these schools is directed toward the education of children, not the preservation of the "educational system."

Several types of schools are attracting the won't learners. These schools provide social and emotional skills as well as academic skills for learners who need help to avoid disaffection, dropping out, gang involvement, and drug abuse. Smaller class sizes, individual curriculum, and experiential learning are useful tools for the won't learner.

This is a book for people who would like to believe that alternative schools can help learners—the won't learners, young people from troubled families, learners who are angry, alienated, bright, bored, lost, and frustrated in large schools.

This book acknowledges that enormous problems *outside* schools do not mean that educators *inside* schools cannot do a better job at helping learners. It is designed to inform and assist those who may be planning a program to answer the cry of youth, many of whom live in the inner city.

The Won't Learners is a book about parents, teachers, community members, and students coming together to make a difference. The book opens by describing the reform movement in education and then gives a brief synopsis of urban education. Chapter 3 presents a description of the teachers who have a passion for teaching, their role in the schools, and how these teachers embrace and plan for the fact that learners bring many common traits to the school, along with differences that make them individuals. These teachers begin where the learners are, not at the front of a curriculum guide.

Chapter 4 looks at the role of the parents who often distrust the system. Inner-city parents who were interviewed reported that their history of working within the system has not been great. A list of what parents want from their children's schools is presented.

In chapter 5, solutions are sought to answer the questions "Where do we begin? How do we journey together?" Bringing together diverse stakeholders, melding our resources, and stretching our minds to embrace new ideas are essential to resolving our problems.

Tips for success and success stories round out chapters 6 and 7. The final chapter reviews the question "Where do we go from here?" and moves us forward toward solutions that will benefit the won't learners and their families. We are challenged to capture the minds of young people by enrolling them in schools they want to attend and that are tailored to their individual needs and interests.

This book will also recommend an alternative way for the reader to look at the won't learner and how we can change the structure of how we teach these young people. Won't learners are bright but often bored young people who need to be able to focus on their interests, values, and learning styles. These students do not work in the classroom because there is no immediate payoff, either in or out of school. The further a student slips behind, the harder it is to summon up the strength to begin to learn. Where education is concerned, there is no punishment that can make a student learn if he or she does not want to. If what is being taught does not satisfy the needs about which a student is currently most concerned, it will make little difference how brilliantly the teacher teaches.

The temper of our youth has become more restless, more critical, more challenging. Added to the challenges of moving through adolescence in a time of great cultural stress are the increasing numbers of both poor children and immigrant arrivals to the United States, creating new and more formidable tasks for the country and its educators.

Meeting America's twenty-first-century challenge is not just a matter of improved teaching of academic content in schools that are now failing. Repairing the torn social fabric that increasingly arrays one group against another will require creating an inclusive social dialogue in which individuals can come to understand diverse experiences and points of view. This suggests not only educating *for* democracy (students needing to learn job skills and good citizenship) but education *as* democracy (education that gives students access to social understanding developed as they actually participate in a pluralistic community, talk together, make decisions, and come to understand multiple views).

Because the economy can no longer absorb many unskilled workers at decent wages, lack of education is increasingly linked to crime and delinquency. Our failure to invest in schools that create adequate life chances for our youth has devastating consequences for individual citizens and for society as a whole.

Growing up humane and caring, and becoming young adults who can appreciate others and take satisfaction in doing things will require schools that model humanity and decency, that cultivate appreciation, and that support learning about things that matter to the people in them. Education should be a source of food for the spirit as well as a means of reaching understanding.

False history thrives because our memories play tricks on us. We forget that discipline, gangs, truancy, low standards, social promotion, and many other issues plagued us in the 1930s, 1940s, 1950s, 1960s, and 1970s. *Why Johnny Can't Read* was a best-seller in the 1960s and we still complain about student ignorance, absence of academic rigor, and parental neglect generation after generation. Teaching, like parenting, feels more like a succession of near misses, almosts, and downright failures.

Youth come to us and want to know what we propose to do about a society that hurts so many of them. There is much to justify in the inquiring attitude of youth. It is clear that many of the old answers are not the right answers. No answer, new or old, is fit for your thought unless it is framed in terms of what you face and what you desire, unless it carries some definite prospect of a practical, down-to-earth solution to your problem. In part, many of our youth do not want to be "well educated" because they cannot even imagine what it is that could be "wantable." The challenge awaits us.

1

A BRIEF HISTORY OF THE
REFORM MOVEMENT IN EDUCATION

We must do the things we think we cannot do. The future belongs to
those who believe in the beauty of their dreams.

—Eleanor Roosevelt

Our failure to educate many children in America's school districts is
one of the great scandals of the twentieth century. Each generation,
children leave school, often by dropping out, without learning the basic
academic skills they need to survive in a complex and changing world.
The cost to society in lost productivity, social support programs, and
crime amounts to billions of dollars each year, and the cost to the individuals in unfulfilled lives is incalculable.

Educators often throw up their hands and blame the larger society.
They point to the serious problems that so many children bring to the
classrooms—social, physical, and emotional problems that make them
appear virtually uneducable. Quite often, educators do not expect much
from students, and those low expectations become self-fulfilling
prophecies. The school's primary function then becomes custodial: to
keep the kids off the streets during the day, and to keep them under
control until they are old enough to leave.

Urban students perform far worse, on average, than children who live
outside central cities on virtually every measure of academic performance.

These students are often denied the resources available to their suburban counterparts. The longer these students stay in school, the wider the gap grows. Today, one out of every four American children (11 million young people) goes to school in an urban district (U.S. Department of Education 1997, 8).

"What's at stake? America's future, nothing short of that," says Gordan Price, former president of the National Urban League. "Where are the employers, entrepreneurs, neighbors, and taxpayers of America in the twenty-first century going to come from? They will be drawn from urban public schools."

Victor Hugo wrote, "There is nothing so powerful as an idea whose time has come." School reform time has arrived. In every part of this country, people have decided that their children are being ill served by the current educational system, and they are opting out. International testing confirms parental intuition. At fourth grade, American children score better in reading and science than most students in other First-World nations, and about average in math. By eighth grade, they are still slightly better in math and science, but falling behind in reading. By twelfth grade, American children are near the bottom in all categories. The conclusion is unmistakable: the longer a child stays in America's schools, the worse he or she performs.

It has been argued that the school reform movement has grown out of the increasing need and demand for better public schools and the desire for parents to choose the school and the programs their children will experience. Educational reform is one part of a more than two-hundred-year push in the United States for expanded educational opportunity.

The American public school was instituted after the War of Independence by political and educational leaders of the time in order to educate the new nation's children to assume the responsibility of citizenship in a democracy. These leaders were deeply concerned with the possibility that the nation would be taken over by a powerful monarchist or else break down from the lack of an informed and responsible leadership.

The reform movement complements the efforts to expand voting rights, to earn a fair wage, and to gain respect. Many educators, frustrated by the current system, believe that public schools can have a significant, positive impact on children, including those who come from troubled families.

In the broadest sense, education includes all those experiences by which intelligence is developed, knowledge is acquired, and character is formed. In a narrower sense, it is the work done by certain agencies and institutions, the home and the school, for the express purpose of educating students. The child is born with latent capacities that must be developed to fit him or her for the activities and duties of life. The meaning of life, therefore, of its purposes and values as understood by the educator, primarily determines the nature of his work. In other words, education is a process of individual becoming, which is the essence of the process of growth taking place in the individual, and the meaning of that growth for the individual.

Education aims at an *ideal* and this, in turn, depends on the view that is taken of a student's destiny, of relationships to peers and the physical world. It can be argued that the *content* of education is found in literature; art and science; and moral, social, and religious principles. However, this content differs greatly in value, both cognitively and culturally. The process used will also influence education. Teaching that is adapted to the needs of the developing mind becomes vitally important for students in all schools.

The work of education normally begins in the home, and then continues in institutions where teachers, curriculum, peers, and the media become as important as parents. The American public school is responsible for educating citizens to develop and maintain a democratic society and for engendering the desire to continue education throughout their lives. In a democratic society, the idea that every person can learn is axiomatic.

To secure efficiency, each school must be properly organized, the teachers must be qualified, and the subjects must be wisely chosen. The school becomes responsible for the intellectual and moral information of those who will later become successful members of society.

Currently, education is defined as that form of social activity whereby, under the direction of educators and by the use of adequate means, the physical, intellectual, and moral powers of the students are so developed as to prepare him or her for the accomplishment of life. It appears that this development is lacking in many students, especially disadvantaged and minority students.

John Dewey, one of the founders of progressive education, developed his theories of education while teaching at the University of Chicago

(1894–1905). Dewey advocated experimenting with and trying out innovative methods in every area of life. He opposed the traditional method of learning by memory under the authority of the teacher. Instead, he believed education should be concerned with manual skills, the interests of students, current problems, and the mind. Dewey also believed that education must include a student's physical and moral well-being, in addition to intellectual development.

The question arises as to the status of education in the United States today. Albert Shanker, American Federation of Teachers president for twenty-three years, said that public education is the glue that has held this country together. Public schools have brought together children of different races, languages, religions, and cultures and have given them a common language and a sense of common purpose. Students are required to learn the old and new basics for survival in today's world. New technology requires teachers and students to tackle them side by side. It appears that successful teachers are excellent communicators as well as fine technicians. These teachers show passion for their work, are clear about what they seek to accomplish, and are more aggressive in communicating values and personal vision statements. What an appeal for our students!

All across the United States, people are concerned about the state of education. Our world has changed. The traditional social structures of family, church, and the neighborhood have been transformed. In many places, crime rates have skyrocketed, powered by increased drug abuse. Unemployment, poverty, and homelessness can be found in every state. These problems cannot be blamed on the schools, but it is important to examine the schools' responses to the crisis of society.

Unfortunately, a look inside many schools might lead one to believe that time has stood still. Students continue to be placed in the same graded classes and taught the same subject matter by the same teaching techniques that teachers used two hundred years ago. Many students continue to learn nineteenth-century answers to twenty-first-century questions. Societal changes challenge schools to accept new responsibilities. The pressures mount for schools to meet the demands of a changing world and to fulfill mandates to educate youth about high-risk topics, such as sex, drugs, and AIDS. Yet the school day is no longer and no different today than it was a decade ago.

Our public schools have been at the center of the social, economic, and technological changes that have swept across the United States since the Brown school-desegregation decisions of 1954–1955, not only in the South and not only for race-related reasons. Every decade has brought new crises, and every decade has brought new reforms.

The 1950s and the 1960s were days of great hope and idealism as many voices proclaimed the good news of unity. However, Russia's launching of *Sputnik* near the end of the Eisenhower era sent shock waves through the nation's defense establishment. With a major infusion of federal funding and federally designed curricula, the public schools initiated a number of innovative programs in mathematics, science, and social studies.

In 1963, Martin Luther King Jr. spoke of his dream of a reconciled society. But then, in that same year, Medgar Evers and President John F. Kennedy were shot to death. In 1965, Malcolm X was killed and, in 1968, Martin Luther King Jr. and Robert F. Kennedy were assassinated. These deaths were a tragic blow for the United States. They were the last public figures in the nation who seemed able to unite people across social and cultural lines to work for social justice. When King and Kennedy were killed within two months of each other, something died in the spirit of many Americans. For many years, we gave up on idealism and the possibility of positive change.

The desegregation struggles of the 1960s and the 1970s made a battleground of many schools, but they also prompted a greatly increased level of federal investment to compensate for generations of neglect at segregated black schools. Head Start, created in the mid-1960s, is one of the most fully documented educational success stories of our time.

In the 1960s and 1970s, students, their parents, and many teachers urged a broadening of curriculum to reflect the multicultural nature of our society. We can only fully appreciate what it means to be human when we welcome the viewpoints of another's culture. By interacting with people of other cultures, we learn more about ourselves as human beings. It turned out, during these years, the Civil Rights movement was contagious, inspiring organized action by various groups—students, faculty, women and girls, disabled students and their parents—to assert their rights to equitable treatment in the schools. Teachers accelerated their campaign to win collective bargaining rights in most areas of the country.

In the years since the 1960s killings, the United States has become a much more fragmented and polarized country, emphasizing self-interest rather than self-sacrifice. A whole generation has grown to adulthood struggling to find an ever-elusive reason to hope.

With the publication of *A Nation at Risk* in 1983, an abrupt halt was called to the "frills" and "dumbing down" instruction the public perceived in the schools. The report beckoned the schools back to basics in no uncertain terms. It ushered in a period of top-down, market-driven school reform proposals. Greater accountability, more rigorous curricula, competency testing for teachers, and higher student scores on standardized tests were the order of the day. "Competition" became the rallying cry.

Because this first wave of the 1980s reform was driven more by political and economic issues than by educational imperatives, and because it was led and legislated from the state level and carried out for the most part without teacher involvement, its impact on students, teachers, and schools was neither positive nor permanent.

During the final days of the 1980s and the early 1990s, images of social justice and freedom were powerful: the Berlin Wall was torn down, a Chinese dissident placed his body in front of a tank, and Nelson Mandela walked to freedom (on his way to becoming president of South Africa). Quite suddenly, a vision for social justice and educational reform was resurrected and a new sense of energy reached many parts of the world.

Equally as suddenly, educators realized that the reforms of the 1980s were doomed from the onset because they asked American public schools to do something they were never designed to do, never did do, and never could do. We have been asking schools to prepare students, all students, for demanding, fast-changing jobs of the future with rigid structures and teaching methods designed for the factories of the early industrial age. We have been asking a nineteenth-century institution to educate people for life in the twenty-first century.

Public schools are nineteenth-century institutions because they were organized around an industrial model that prevailed at the turn of the century. Mass production sought to reduce as many elements of the manufacturing process as possible to simple, repetitive tasks that would be handled by workers who were easily trained. Industry, given the complexity of new production processes and the need to introduce new products more frequently, had abandoned the old hierarchical structures. They decentralized and reorganized around teams of workers, each responsible for organizing and carrying out their assignments. They adopted more flexible work schedules and developed new standards for quality control.

What is our legacy from these past decades of crisis and reform? Undoubtedly, each wave of change has made its mark. We have progressed past the time when multicultural education meant decorating the school with pictures of dead African American heroes in an annual celebration of Black History Month. Textbooks and school curriculum today reflect the social and ethnic diversity of our society.

The improvement of the teaching profession has been sustained and the development of mature bargaining relationships between employee organizations and school districts has created more democratic school governing structures throughout the country.

The struggles continue. Many teachers and students in the predominantly black, Hispanic, and American Indian schools of the nation's inner cities are living with the "savage inequalities" described so well by Jonathan Kozol: schools without libraries, science labs with little or no lab equipment, windowless rooms, leaking ceilings, peeling paint, elimination of course offerings, and budget cuts.

The shifting currents of educational reform over the past fifty years reveal the stress of institutional response to the constant push and pull of often opposing forces in our society.

What we have inherited in our public school system is a national treasure, a vast, sprawling, outdated, but still resilient institution. As we work to make it better for all children who are entering life in the twenty-first century, we are building on strength, not weakness. We are also building upon lessons learned from the successes and failures of the past. A school's success should be viewed over a long period of time, measured in terms of student achievement, professional growth and leadership, ethical conduct, parental relations, and school reputation.

No reform movement, no matter how well intended or how brilliant in theory, can be successfully "grafted onto" the educational system by outside authorities without regard for the unique culture of each school. No reform measure will endure as an organic part of the school program without the leadership and commitment of teachers in all stages of its design and implementation. And no reform measure will be effective if its aim is to improve uniformity in teaching and learning. Students come in infinite variety; few will be responsive to standard-issue instruction. What is needed, and what is emerging today, is an authentic approach to school renewal, one that is school-based, faculty-led, and student-centered. Shifting authority, shared leadership, integration of research and practice, and building school or home connections are keys to educational reform.

What was the state of public education at the end of the year 2000? Curriculum wars have endured for at least one hundred years. The debate about what should be taught and to whom erupted in 1893 when the Committee of Ten espoused a liberal education of the highest quality for all students. The curriculum wars continued throughout the twentieth century as the "progressives" endorsed such practices as vocational education, social efficiency, mental measurement, child centeredness, and life adjustment, much to the chagrin of the traditionalists who wanted schools to remain as they were. The wars are now surfacing in movements such as multiculturalism, constructivism, and experience-based education.

According to D. Ravitch in her book *Left Back: A Century of Failed School Reforms* (2000), all these movements have pulled schools away from providing an academic education for all students and have dumbed down the curriculum, resulting in inequity and mediocre achievement. She writes, "If there is a lesson to be learned from the river of ink that was spilled in the education disputes of the twentieth century, it is that anything in education that is labeled a 'movement' should be avoided like the plague" (453).

Caught in the divisive dualism that pervades our politics and media, Ravitch sees history as a battle between traditional and progressive forces. Traditionalists are those who believe in academics and high standards, and progressives must be everyone else.

However, noted authorities, who are looking backward and forward at the movements in education in which they have been most immersed during their careers, find that the future possibilities for schools stir the imagination.

In America today, alternative education is on the front burner of educational reform. Historian Ronald Takaki (1999) reminds us to know history and to share it with others. In this manner, we can include diverse voices from the past.

A brief history of the alternative education movement deserves being mentioned at this point.

Following *A Nation at Risk*, most local school districts in the United States began to evaluate performance standards and to stress accountability. New needs began to emerge; new programs were tried. This became an effort to cope with changing life conditions, social mobility, and new expectations. One of these "new" programs was the alternative school. However, much of what is regarded as new or innovative in education has a long historical record. Most of the current practices designed to improve instruction were tried, in some form, by progressive educators. For example, individualized instruction, team teaching, open classrooms, schools without walls, work-study programs, nongraded schools, competency-based programs, and alternative schools were all tried in some form or another by progressive educators in the 1930s. Progressives ruled education in the 1930s. They believed that each child was unique and that there were many styles of learning. In some ways, progressive schools were similar to most modern-day alternative schools.

Many progressive schools of the era incorporated John Dewey's educational principles calling for the transformation of education. Dewey viewed the school as the agent of social change that must use society's transition into the Industrial Age. Dewey's solution was to change the school into an embryonic community that would include the study of occupations as well as art, history, and science. More importantly, the child would learn intellectual responsibility by selecting and implementing a plan of work and would receive guidance when errors were made. Methods suggested by Maria Montessori were also considered. She believed that children mature at different rates and this should be the basis of the educational system.

New needs began to emerge after World War II. Critics began to condemn progressive education, child-centered programs, and permissive practices. A new conservation in education sprang up. With the increase in industrialism in the United States, schools were modeled after businesses. Schools then became factories, processing students in much the same way that an automobile is processed. Anonymity and detachment became pervasive for students, staff, and community.

More needs emerged in the 1950s. George Dennison established the first "street school," an alternative educational program for minority students from low-income families in New York City's Lower East Side. Half of his students came from public schools where they had been given such labels as "severe learning and behavior problems," "incorrigible," "antisocial," and "gang oriented." Dennison responded to the needs of those who had been cast off by parents and society. Schools in the early 1950s strove to develop a sense of belonging. Some schools began to individualize curricula. However, by the mid to late 1950s, public fear of lowered academic standards, triggered by the *Sputnik* launch, put a halt to alternative programs.

We can also trace the roots of the current alternative thrust to the Civil Rights movement of the 1960s. As desegregation gained momentum, public schools were boycotted. This led to the creation of "freedom schools" in storefronts and churches. For many, the freedom schools offered a glimpse of alternative education designed to meet their needs. This included caring adults, new curriculum, and more community involvement.

In 1967, Herbert Kohl created a curriculum from his students' experiences and his own imagination. Kohl claimed success in combining creativity and relevant experiences with academic achievement. The nation's interest in school reform abated in the 1970s, but there has been a steady increase in alternative schools. Success was cited with youngsters who had previously detested school. Throughout the 1970s and 1980s, alternative schools have been called on to solve a variety of our nation's ills, ranging from crime and delinquency to youth unemployment.

There was a renewed interest in what was termed alternative reform in the 1990s. Minnesota was the first state in the nation to adopt a form of alternative education called "charter schools." In 1991, charter school legislation allowed interested community members to create and manage a school. A public school district, an education district, an accredited institution of higher learning, the state, and most recently, some nonprofit organizations can sponsor a charter school.

Joe Nathan, director of the Center for School Change at the University of Minnesota Humphrey Institute of Public Affairs and a national expert in educational reform, says that charter schools bring together three powerful forces that are central to the American experience: choice, entrepreneurial spirit, and accountability. People want choice in how children are educated, want the opportunity to realize dreams, and want accountability.

A charter school is a public school, thus no tuition. Any student may enroll. Like other public schools, a charter school receives state funds, must meet state education and graduation standards, and must be accountable to a state department of education.

"Charter schools give choice and kids deserve choice," says Steve Dess, executive director of the Minnesota Association of Charter Schools. Many learners are attending charter schools as an alternative to traditional education.

The reality is that American schools in the 1990s continue to have large numbers of students who drop out because they are unable to compete, bored, poorly adjusted, or are merely uninterested in the courses. Numerous school systems are attempting to offer alternative education in an effort to meet the needs of students for whom the regular educational program is unsatisfactory. Alternative education, like the struggling student, is not a new concept, although its forms continue to change.

Why do kids with such self-defeating attitudes do so well in alternative educational systems? For one thing, kids bounce back quickly when teachers and other staff members respect them as individuals who have unique talents and abilities. For another, the kids understand that rigorous standards and high expectations are signs that people have faith in them.

"My new teachers keep telling me I'm smart and I can pass even my toughest classes," says a ninth grader who just enrolled in an alternative school across town from his previous high school. "I might make it in this school. . . . I just got a B on my science test. . . . I'm starting to believe in myself."

Most alternative schools today are based on beliefs that go back to the 1960s and 1970s, when such schools started to figure significantly in the educational landscape. Then, as now, alternative schools sought to break away from the systems and structures that characterize most traditional schools. These schools often depart from tradition in such ways as giving students choices in setting their daily schedule, allowing them to work at their own pace, and providing advice and counseling. At many alternative schools, students work with their teachers to tailor individual programs, taking courses on a flexible schedule instead of rigid semesters.

Alternative programs need to include a rich mixture of ingredients to make their programs successful. Some nonnegotiable ingredients in the mix include a small student population, individualized instruction, flexible scheduling, peer counseling, caring and competent teachers and administrators, an interesting and relevant curriculum, and a homelike atmosphere. Alternative schools can then stir their own ingredients into the mix. (Extra features such as mentoring programs, parenting classes, attendance contracts, and school-to-work/career programs are dependent on the student population.)

What kinds of students need these schools? In a paper presented to the American Educational Research Association, Susan Barnes and Jane Stewart described common characteristics of alternative education students in terms of their previous school setting and their school attitude and performance. The researchers found that the students had attended large schools where they were placed in low or nonacademic tracks. They associated with dropouts, viewed teachers and principals as unsupportive, and did not participate in school activities. What's more, these students generally received low grades, were habitually absent, were suspended from school, had negative attitudes toward learning, failed a grade, and got into trouble both in and out of school.

Challenging as it might seem, alternative schools are turning such kids around. According to the kids who attend alternative schools, it's easier to strive for success when the teachers work with them individually, often coaching and supporting them through difficult stages. It's also easier to succeed when teachers show that they genuinely care.

Believing in the kids is the theory behind the alternative school programs. These students are a profile of the "won't learners." Cicchelli and Marcus (1995) call them "driftouts" because they tend to fade out of their regular school's mainstream into low tracks and dead-end courses before they actually drop out. Over time, these kids develop a mirror image of the school's attitude. They see themselves as losers who can't do anything right. Allowing alternative programs to raise the bar without ensuring the opportunity to learn is simply a way of exacerbating the disparities that currently exist.

As we look at educational reform and where we have come from, we can summarize the role of alternative education since 1950 as having

- Developed basic skills for vocational preparation not offered in the traditional public schools
- Concern for improvement of students' self-concept, more interactions, and allowances for greater awareness by pupils of who they are
- Emphasized the development of individual talent and uniqueness
- An understanding and encouragement of cultural plurality and diversity
- Prepared students for various roles in our society (consumer, voter, critic, parent, spouse, etc.)
- Been responsive to the needs within their communities
- Provided a flexible and more responsive reaction to planned evolution and change
- Designed curriculum that students feel are more relevant to the needs and desires of what they want to learn
- Been more humane to students and teachers, with smaller classes, fewer rules, and fewer bureaucratic constraints
- Provided a choice
- Accepted students who are not suited for traditional schools

In an effort to understand what educational reform is all about, we must participate in a dialogue about diverse and similar experiences of the students in our classrooms. Lasting reforms must reflect a deep-rooted social concern for democracy, for equity, or for preparing students to lead fulfilling adult lives. Reforms that have not lasted have often attempted to change teaching practices without being well understood or accepted by the teachers who are most knowledgeable about how classrooms work.

Teachers grapple with questions about what improves learning. Where and how does this idea work? Do we have evidence from other classrooms that change will promote learning? How does it fit with our knowledge and experience of what engages students? If we are going to effect change, we must understand that instructional strategies are values-led and people-centered.

Look at the example of the kindergarten. The nation was industrializing rapidly and urban living for families, particularly immigrant and poor families, had become more difficult. Kindergartens were introduced to public schools in the 1870s; before that, private kindergartens were aimed at middle- and upper-income families in the Midwest and New England areas. Public kindergartens were introduced as a way of "preserving" childhood before kids encountered the rigor of grammar school or high school, as well as teaching parents how to live in the cities. Kindergartens slowly spread, so that by the late 1960s, kindergarten was a mainstay.

This gradual growth came not only from the formation of constituencies but also from a general belief that the earlier a child learns in formal situations, the better chance the child will have at academic and financial success. Public schools have always been looked at as an escalator for social mobility and parents have always wanted to give their children an edge. This notion of an early start gradually became fixed, and no one today would think of banning kindergarten or preschool.

Another example of reform that has remained is the growth of high schools and the development of "comprehensive" high schools that provide different curricula for diverse students. Until the turn of the twentieth century, education for most children ended after eighth grade. By World War I, the comprehensive high school had been introduced and enrollment expanded. Labor laws kept children in school longer. The democratic belief that every child has a different employment future pushed school administrators to provide a different curriculum for diverse students. The high school was called comprehensive because it had a job future in mind for every child coming to school, and was seen as a very democratic institution because of the equality of economic opportunity that was presumed to be embedded in the different curricula.

The reforms that have the least potential for sticking are those that try to bring about changes in teaching, primarily because those innovations are often proposed by policymakers and officials who know little about classrooms.

An obvious example is what is going on with the teaching of reading. People were led to believe that many classrooms were being taught through whole language because there was a lot of talk about this method among educators, in journals, and in the media. Actually, most classrooms were not teaching reading through whole language; most teachers were using combinations of phonics and whole language. The evidence about the takeover of reading instruction by whole language enthusiasts was very slim, but it was a great talking point for public officials who wanted to make a major issue out of it. We need to remember that there is an important distinction between policy talk and policy implementation.

Schools reflect the cultural, social, and economic changes of the larger society. When new proposals collide with the complex reality of teaching and learning, there are often countermovements and the schools must adapt again.

One challenge to school reform lies in the paradox of creating a common vision among people with different beliefs and assumptions about education. Thomas Hatch (1998) describes people involved in a school reform effort as "jugglers who have been learning their craft on their own and who suddenly had to figure out how to toss the balls to one another." Sustaining schoolwide reform programs past the initial stage of enthusiasm is one of the biggest problems that schools face.

As the popularity of the reform movement grows, schools and educators demand more analytical information. Now that a diverse mix of schoolwide programs exists, the focus of researchers and educators is on implementation. As we determine why some models and schools are successful while others often struggle, we must ensure that the success of all students remains in the forefront. School reform does not just relate to reading and writing. It relates to the lives and the environment of the students.

Ultimately, only three things matter about educational reform: (1) Does it improve important rather than superficial aspects of student learning? (2) Does it have length? Is it sustainable over long periods of time? (3) Does it have breadth? Can it be extended beyond a few schools, networks, or showcase initiatives? Successful school reform is a Picasso, not a Rembrandt. It approaches change, not from one or two dimensions, but like a cubist painter, from all three at once.

What leads to success in the three dimensions of educational reform? How do the three dimensions interact and what strategies secure progress?

Depth: Social and emotional understanding. Increasingly, educational reformers want more than improved achievement results. They want deep, powerful, high-performance learning for understanding that prepares all learners to participate in today's society.

Learning for understanding is not just cognitive and psychological. It involves more than constructivism, multiple intelligences, metacognition, or problem-based learning. Deep learning is also cultural and emotional. Students, especially our won't learners, must contextualize learning in what they have learned before, in what other teachers are teaching them, and in their own cultures and lives.

In addition to establishing cultural connections, teachers have to create emotional bonds with and among students. These bonds are the building blocks of empathy, tolerance, and civic duty. Emotional understanding—the ability to read instantaneously how well students are learning or are engaged in learning—is a foundation of the standards agenda, not a sidebar to it. Without strong bonds and sustained relationships with students, emotional understanding and learning standards suffer. When learners are diverse and demanding, educators must be responsive to students' varied cultures, inclusive of their own ideas in defining learning targets or sharing assessment criteria, and ready to involve families and communities to bring learning to higher levels.

As we look at reform, we need to ask ourselves how we become fluent in other cultures. One way this happens is when we live outside our comfort zones and relate in significant ongoing ways to people who are different from us. Curtis DeYoung, author of *Coming Together* (1995), says that our fluency expands as we listen to and live with people from diverse settings. This helps us gain points of reference for communicating cross-culturally. If possible, we need to be mentored by persons who are from cultures or racial groups different from our own. We must look for a greater awareness of our similarities. Not only do the powerful need to understand the experience of the oppressed, the powerful need to fathom empowerment.

Length: Sustaining changes over time. Educational change requires more than strategies. It also requires ways to anticipate and overcome obstacles to sustain change over time. Leadership succession, staff recruitment and retention, size, district policy, and community support are critical elements if a school is to sustain its innovative character.

Breadth: Extending the model. Sustainability does not simply mean that something can last. It also addresses how particular initiatives can be developed without compromising the development of others in the surrounding environment, now and in the future. Sustainable change is more than a question for individual schools; it extends to whole districts, states, and nations.

Schools and districts are not all alike. Variations can exist in the social and cultural characteristics of students, the extent to which schools involve teachers in policy development, the quality of leadership, and past experiences with change. Transplanting an initiative that has been successful in one district or group of schools to others is difficult. Transplanted initiatives soon become transformed ones, diverging sharply from initial intentions.

This is known as the challenge of "scaling up." It entails developing ambitious models for school reform by building networks of technical assistance and school-to-school support to ever-expanding numbers of schools that freely choose to implement the models. A proliferation of such models seeks to change structures, cultures, and learning conditions of schools by using adventurous volunteer schools and districts as catalysts to scale up reform across wider systems.

Scaling-up strategies have had uneven success. A review of twenty-four U.S. models of schoolwide change in 1999 by the American Institute for Research found that only three demonstrated strongly positive efforts on student achievement. Interestingly, these models mainly had a narrow, prescribed, and somewhat conservative instructional focus on literacy and numeracy skills or on direct instruction. They provide breadth without depth.

Efforts at districtwide change that show promising signs of success have a persistent emphasis on teaching, learning, and student performance; on partnerships that share and develop expertise; on the stringent selection of teachers and leaders; and on assessment and accountability factors.

Touchstones for change do exist and school reform can become three-dimensional. We need to focus on deep learning, not just superficial performance results. The educational battle against poverty, disadvantage, and racial inequality involves making broad connections with families, and dramatic changes to the structure and curricula of schools, to contextualize learning in a deep way, and to create conditions for it to occur. Yet this agenda is being pervasively whittled down to more specific preoccupations with literacy, numeracy, and cognitive standards. Of course, literacy, numeracy, and standards are part of a deeper learning agenda but are not a substitute for it. Better achievement results do not necessarily mean deeper learning.

We also must use model schools to reculture, not just to restructure, the system. Deep learning demands changes. Schools typically instigate this shift with a shock-and-copy strategy. Teachers become distrustful, angry, and jealous if they feel that the district rams a particular model down their throats. Model schools often work best not as blueprints to copy in the short term, but as places to grow systemwide cultures and leadership for the long run.

The goal of educational reform must be to establish not just islands and archipelagoes of improvement but entire continents of change. Critical points of policy context repeatedly sabotage this goal. If and when particular governments alter these factors, subsequent shifts in political control will probably only reverse them. In the end, educators would do better to capture the public imagination on which governments depend by making their practice and improvement efforts highly visible and by helping create a broad social movement for large-scale, deep, and sustainable transformation in public education that will benefit all students.

Deep, sustainable, and scaled-up reform is not achieved by mandate, by shock-and-copy strategies, or by other quick fixes. In fact, many educators cite school reform as a "twenty-first-century vision of education, a way to embrace the changes that lie ahead by creating change in our educational system."

Expecting to make full progress on all three dimensions mentioned earlier (length, depth, and breadth) at once is unrealistic. Our current three-dimensional reform is an ambitious, complex, and trying, as well as controversial—a balancing act.

What is effective education for students who have historically been given fewer opportunities to achieve? What are the strategies that lead to higher achievement and fuller enjoyment of learning for all students? Alternative schools can be a lifeline for the kids traditional schools can't reach. They can become havens for the kids who truly have nowhere else to go.

The true test of our democracy, and of our public schools, is the way in which we respond to the crying need of the children who live in the nation's poorest neighborhoods, wherever they are. This is not to say that only poverty-stricken kids have problems and needs. Young people of every social and economic class suffer from the stresses of contemporary life. It is the responsibility of our schools to be sensitive and responsive to the particular needs of all children, rich, poor, and in between. We must act on the principle that all children are valuable and that all children can learn.

The task before our schools is to prepare every child in America for the challenging world of the twenty-first century. This world demands problem-solving skills, the ability to work with other people, and the capacity to continue learning throughout life.

Reform becomes possible when individuals with different roles, students, teachers, school administrators, and policymakers interact around a shared concern for student learning.

Human energy is the key to school reform. Although money is widely used to symbolize the nutrients schools need to grow, money simply buys time. Focused human energy is what school reform requires.

It is now time for schools to change. It is no longer possible to run an effective system of public education under the old values of centralized authority, standardization, and bureaucratic accountability. The "thinking society" of the twenty-first century can no longer be content with graduates trained to take in and recycle information handed out by teachers and other authority figures. Today's students must be taught to think for themselves and generate new information. We cannot allow our won't learners to fall by the wayside.

2

A BRIEF DESCRIPTION
OF URBAN EDUCATION

If you have your language and your culture and you're not ashamed
of them, then you know who you are.

—Maria Urquides

Exaggerating the educational crisis in America's cities would be difficult. Words like scandal, failure, corruption, and despair echo in the
pages of the nation's newspapers. These words aptly describe many urban districts and the schools within them.

To be sure, some big-city schools and districts evoke words like hero-
ism, commitment, innovation, and success, but these remain exceptions.
Such islands of achievement serve to make even less tolerable the
oceans of failure that surround them. If one school can succeed under
the worst conditions, with the most needy children, how can others be
permitted to fail?

Urban children are often saddled with burdens of crime, poverty, and
unemployment that most of us cannot begin to appreciate. Their cities
have deteriorated and their lives are often bleak. Urban youth live in a
culture where schools, studying, and homework are secondary. Test
scores, dropout rates, and low attendance rates at colleges all indicate a
severe failure of our education system for the inner-city student.

Many of the intractable problems that plague urban schools are deeply rooted in the poverty, unemployment, crime, racism, and human despair that pervade the neighborhoods around them. Too often, teachers and administrators are asked to solve problems that the public and its leaders in state houses have lacked the time to tackle.

Urban children often come from low-income families. Studies have shown that these children are more likely to die in infancy and early childhood, suffer serious illness, become pregnant during their teen years, and drop out of school. They are also less likely to continue education beyond high school. Violence, drugs, street crimes, and unemployment constitute social problems that the public expects schools to help alleviate, if not eliminate.

Some urban districts are rising to meet the enormous challenges before them. Here and there, test scores are climbing, dropout rates are falling, order is returning, and children are learning. Invariably, in these pockets of success, we find bold leadership, imaginative initiatives, and extraordinary efforts by individual teachers and administrators. However, the problems still overwhelm the progress. Urban schools are fighting a battle they cannot win without support from local, state, and federal political leaders and from voters and taxpayers outside the cities.

Today, one out of every four American children—11 million young people—goes to school in an urban district. Consider then:

- Urban students are far less likely to graduate on time than nonurban students are.
- Some 43 percent of minority students attend urban schools. Most attend schools in which more than half the students are from low-income families and are predominately children of color.
- A majority of urban students fails to meet minimum standards on national tests in about half the states.
- The poorest students are at the greatest risk.
- Schools in urban districts tend to be larger, have higher truancy rates, and have less involvement from parents than other schools.
- Inner-city districts are twice as likely as nonurban ones to hire teachers who have no license or maintain an emergency or temporary license.

When people talk about the problems in public education, they are talking about big-city schools, especially the ones that serve low-income children. Urban students perform far worse, on average, than children who live outside central cities on virtually every measure of educational performance. The longer these urban children remain in school, the wider the gap grows.

City districts are overwhelmed by politics, a rapid turnover in administrators, inadequate resources, shortages of teachers, disengaged or angry parents, and apathy from state lawmakers.

The causes of these problems cannot all be laid at the feet of the districts. Since World War II, America's big cities have struggled with the middle-class flight to suburbia and the loss of manufacturing jobs. Since 1970, neighborhoods in city after city have collapsed under the weight of poverty and neglect.

"The children of the inner city are a minority isolated in many ways from mainstream American society," William L. Taylor, a civil rights lawyer, said in a 1997 speech at Stanford University.

The numbers tell a sad and alarming story: Most fourth graders who live in cities in the United States cannot read and understand a simple children's book, and most eighth graders cannot use arithmetic to solve a practical problem. At the high school level, slightly more than half of inner-city students fail to graduate in four years. Even those who do graduate and end up with a diploma are unprepared for the workplace or college. Somehow, simply *being* in an urban school seems to drag performance down.

The biggest challenge facing American cities and their school systems is concentrated poverty. In low-income neighborhoods, the deck is stacked against children from the moment they are born. The odds are higher that they will have lower than normal birth weights, lack access to regular medical care, live in a household headed by a single mother, become a victim of crime, have a parent who never finished high school, become pregnant before reaching adulthood, and drop out of school. Even the harshest critics of urban school systems recognize that they did not get there on their own. Economic changes, including the astonishing geographic spread of inner-city ghettos, mean educators are often swimming against a powerful tide of concentrated poverty.

By the time many urban learners reach secondary school, they have fallen so far behind that it is virtually impossible for them to catch up.

Students in the ninth grade are reading at the third and fourth grade levels. Unfortunately, that is not all that students are suffering from. Many urban learners are sidetracked by early sexual activity, drug and alcohol abuse, and gang membership. Some are parents themselves. Many work after school and on weekends. And, for too many students who live in poverty, there seems little point in studying when the prospect for college or a high-paying job seems remote.

The structure of schools themselves tends to make them resistant to change. Often, these schools are organized into academic departments and bound by the external requirements of graduation standards and college admission. Many are impersonal factories where students and teachers have little real contact. As long as our urban public schools remain impersonal structures that alienate both students and parents, they will continue to promote poor attendance, poor conduct, and high dropout rates among the large numbers of minority students who attend them.

A sense of urgency about educational difficulties in the inner city permeates conversations about education in the media, statehouse, community, and classroom. Everyone believes in the value of public education. No one buys the idea that because our schools face daunting challenges, the nation should scale back its ambitions for educating young people. But unless our inner-city schools become the architects of change, they will become the victims of change.

Inner-city schools are also challenged by an enrollment boom, limited institutional flexibility, new competition for students, eroding public trust, a graying teaching force, growing numbers of immigrant and poor children, and troubling evidence about institutional effectiveness.

The challenges facing urban schools are no longer technical issues about how to manage enrollment, allocate revenues, or even increase achievement. They are much more difficult problems, what Ronald Heifetz, director of the Leadership Educational Project at Harvard University, defines as "adaptive challenges": about how to lead when conditions change, expectations remain high, cynicism grows, and options appear limited.

Public education in urban areas is in deep trouble: Dropout rates hover above 25 percent, truancy is common, violence is a perpetual threat, students struggle for basic literacy (often without success), a great deal of teaching is uninspired, and the physical condition of many schools borders on the scandalous. Urban schools are unprepared to cope with the challenges they face in terms of the number and type of students who need both education and preparation for life. For example, the total population of children in New York City, Los Angeles, Chicago, Houston, and Philadelphia is in excess of 4 million. Many of these children live in poverty, sometimes extreme poverty. The magnitude of this problem is illustrated by the following: Four out of every 270 Americans is a low-income child living in one of the country's five largest cities; most of these children come from minority backgrounds and the overwhelming number of these children attends or will attend public schools (U.S. Census Bureau 1999).

Using New York City as an example of the catastrophic situation facing low-income inner-city children provides a sense of what these statistics mean.

- One out of every four people living in New York City is a child.
- Every day, 373 babies are born; of these babies, 4 will die before their first birthday, 181 are born into poverty, 38 are born to teenage parents, 45 are born to mothers with inadequate prenatal care, and 34 are born with low birth weight.
- Every day, 711,000 children live in poverty.
- Every day, 9,600 children are homeless.
- Every day, 51 percent of elementary and middle school students read below grade level.
- Every day, 144 children are reported abused or neglected.
- Every week, 11,393 children use mental health services.
- Every twelve hours, a young person under twenty-five years of age is murdered.

In the last twenty years, the collision course between the failing school system and the new student population has become increasingly more evident. Although some reforms have made a positive impact, the condition of urban education remains desolate, and there is a growing sense that piecemeal reform does not and will not have a lasting impact. As a result, some reformers are calling for a radical change in how schools and school systems are governed.

We are witnessing an explosion of interest in creating new types of schools and in giving parents the power to choose among them because there is no "one best school" for every child. It has been argued that parents who are given choices are more likely to be involved in and committed to the chosen school. Choice can include private schools, residential schools, choice across districts, second chance programs for dropouts, alternative schools, magnet schools, and charter schools.

"Choice" is a word that captures the belief that public schools are failing because they are bureaucratic, controlled by teachers' unions, and incapable of meaningful reform. Choice reformers believe that empowering families with educational options will liberate the energy and creativity latent in the system. Choice captures many different types of reforms, from vouchers (which deregulate public education) to intradistrict choice (which allows students to choose schools within their public school district) without challenging any of the assumptions about the organization of public education.

What follows is an overview of school choice.

To understand school choice, it is important to return to *Brown vs. Board of Education*. In 1954, the Supreme Court ruled that racial segregation could not be constitutionally supported on the basis of the "separate but equal" principle affirmed in *Plessey vs. Ferguson* (1896), an earlier Supreme Court case. In effect, the Court found that separate was not equal and that minority students in the United States were being deprived of their rights to equal protection under the law. The Brown decision radically altered American public education. By mandating that public schools be racially integrated, it implicitly called for the redesign of public education. However, despite the Court's decision, de facto segregation has continued, North and South, because American neighborhoods are still segregated by race and class. In fact, the first choice schools were "white flight" academies. In panic to avoid sending their children to school with African American students, white parents in both the North and the South withdrew from the public school system and established private academies that were often indirectly funded by public funds.

By the 1960s, it was becoming increasingly apparent that de facto segregation was, in the words of the federally established Kerner Commission, creating two societies, one poor and minority, the other white and affluent. Numerous studies called for the reform of public education in the inner cities, and several articulate critics testified to the damage that public education was doing to minority students. Jonathan Kozol (1991) mapped out the terrain of pain with startling clarity, and writers such as Michael Harrington (1962) showed Americans that poverty continued to exist throughout the country.

When Lyndon Johnson became president, he sought to build the "Great Society" by creating an environment of equal opportunity, material abundance, and social justice. Along with Reverend Martin Luther King Jr., Johnson and other liberals attempted to integrate the country through court decisions and legislation. The passions aroused by the war in Indochina effectively destroyed the political consensus required to make the "Great Society" a reality. In addition, the Black Power movement challenged the integrationist ideal by arguing for separation of the races and racial pride. The objective was to gain control of schools in black communities so that members could teach African American-centered curricula and the values of the local community. In the minds of Black Power advocates, public schools were little more than an extension of white power, white ideology, and white control. Attacking the educational status quo on another front, a number of white educational reformers were simultaneously criticizing the public school system as morally and intellectually deadening. Many of these critics formed alternative schools in New York City, Chicago, Los Angeles, and other major cities.

In the meantime, conservative economist Milton Friedman (1962) was arguing that by its very nature public education was an affront to the ideals of freedom and marketplace accountability. In essence, Friedman laid the groundwork for an alternative model of school governance that emphasized parent choice and was based on the belief that markets are better arbiters of personal and social good than are state-mandated regulations.

Public education in the 1970s was experimental. The open classroom was idealized, new curricula were touted, "discovery" learning was introduced, and teachers' unions, under the leadership of Albert Shanker, became increasingly powerful. Public education seemed to be entering an era of optimism.

In 1980, the conservative coalition led by President Ronald Reagan challenged the existing consensus by arguing against state power for market power. Choice made its first national political major break-through at the National Governor's Conference in 1986. In their report *Time for Results*, the governors said, "If we first implement choice, true choice among public schools, we unlock the values of competition in the marketplace. Schools that compete for students, teachers, and dollars will, by virtue of the environment, make these changes that will allow them to succeed."

In sum, school choice is a "hot" educational, political, and social issue. As dissatisfaction with the public schools continues to grow, more and more people are turning to choice to provide real reform. Unlike many school reforms, choice has caught the public imagination and prompted policymakers to work with legislators, business contacts, and educators. Choice is a national movement, focused in urban areas, changing not only the way American education is organized but also how Americans think about education. The impact on urban school reform has com-pelled educators and other education stakeholders to rethink and re-design how public schools are organized, evaluated, and supported.

There is little doubt that the monolith of urban public education is being entirely transformed. There has been wide experimentation with magnet schools and a host of other nontraditional approaches to educa-tion. Some of these experiments have proven to be exciting from an ed-ucational reform point of view. Others have turned out to be less fruit-ful. Most children involved live in urban areas and attend neighborhood schools. Remember, reform can be motivated from a number of differ-ent sources, perhaps the most lasting of which are from those teachers, parents, community members, and administrators who, through experi-ence and dedication, arrive at a vision that is grounded in the lives of in-ner-city youth. It should be noted, however, that without choice, a child's educational experience and, hence, economic and social futures are con-strained by the vagaries of chance. Children's opportunities are influ-enced by the neighborhood that their parents choose to live in, or are forced to live in, and by the quality of the schools in that neighborhood. Choice provides exit from these controlling circumstances and, to that degree, provides opportunities that might not otherwise exist for many children.

There is always a flip side to a reform movement. Some educators and parents believe choice is not a reform silver bullet. These policymakers point out that it is highly unlikely that students will be able to travel long distances to attend schools of their choice in large urban systems without restructuring and refinancing public transportation. They also cite that many children will not be able to attend their first, second, or even third school of choice.

Another limitation is that accountability is very difficult in an open choice system. Further, there is little compelling evidence that school choice is directly related to higher student achievement.

Finally, these policymakers believe there is a huge underclass of the permanently poor. This group includes whites who are as shut out of the economic system as are so many African Americans, American Indians, Hispanic, and Asian populations. What is the likelihood that this population could benefit by school choice? These policymakers believe good schools for all children will be achieved through financial equity, prepared professionals, and high standards and purpose, not by school choice.

Nowhere are the problems and needs of children as great as in inner cities, where the lives of so many children are in disorder. We cannot escape the already mentioned problems of unemployment, crime, child abuse and neglect, and addiction to drugs and alcohol.

Amongst this neglect and despair aimed at children in the inner cities is every reason to hope and work for improvement. Children are remarkably resilient; they respond readily to caring adults and a supportive community. We must rekindle hope for remaking inner-city education into a system that fosters resilience and educational success for these urban communities.

How about building on urban learners' experiences? Finding out about children's experiences outside of school can unearth valuable information about interests and skills, providing the foundation for classroom activities that motivate and engage the minds of urban learners.

"Does it count?" That is the first thing students will ask about any educational program, the late Albert Shanker used to remind policymakers. The answer had better be an unequivocal "Yes" or chances are slim that students will achieve at high levels.

Urban students are capable, motivated, resilient learners, able to build on their cultural strengths. We must reject perceptions of urban children as at-risk, lacking abilities, unmotivated, and culturally deprived.

The war on poverty lives! In order to best service inner-city learners, many areas are advocating a wish list for students: all-day preschool for three-year-olds, after-hours programs that use school buildings as community centers, classes for parents, child care for teenage
mothers, legal assistance for children, educational sports leagues, and
even school-based dentists. School reform does not just relate to reading and writing. It relates to the horrible conditions in which children
live. Students who arrive at school hungry will not learn as well as
those who are well fed.

Our challenge is to demystify the process of learning and help students understand how their knowledge and daily experiences relate to
the curriculum content. (One teacher, instead of being preoccupied
with identifying prior knowledge about volcanoes, put the students
ahead of his content and drew from them experiences that were in
many ways analogous to volcanic eruptions. Students were asked to
describe, from their own experiences, how they have been exposed to
eruptions. Responses ranged from eruptions of acne to eruptions of
laughter or anger. In each example, students described various aspects
of an eruption that became the basis for making connections to the
curriculum content.)

Success for inner-city children means excellence in school and love
in the midst of desperation. Caring is most likely the greatest reason
for the success of the students attending inner-city schools. Educating
is an individualized, lifelong process of learning, discovering, accepting, and trying.

Many successful inner-city schools are providing a nontraditional
environment driven by student needs. These schools provide the education and the skills necessary for students to achieve self-sufficiency
and to become contributing participants within their communities.
Our task is to provide a supportive environment that motivates and allows students to recognize windows of opportunity and to reach their
educational and career goals. Curriculum is shaped to meet the needs
of the students and to focus on their learning styles. Effective teachers understand the many behaviors taking place in the classroom and
react appropriately.

In light of environment, cultural diversity within urban settings has become a subject of lively debate. The challenges for people with different

cultural perspectives living and working together are being discussed in university classrooms and on street corners, often with tension, fear, and misunderstanding. We have a growing number of people identifying themselves as biracial, interracial, multiracial, or multicultural.

Urban education is multicultural education. It is important to note that our cultural and social settings shape the rules or methods we use for interpretation. The growing diversity in our world represents more than just racial and cultural differences. The gap between rich and poor continues to widen. Men and women are struggling to make sense out of changing gender roles. Our world is experiencing a broad range of philosophical outlooks and educational attainments. As a result of changing demographics and enhanced communication systems, people are increasingly interacting with each other. The United States has become a microcosm of heterogeneous perspectives from around the world. Many are settling in our urban areas. For many, these extensive changes have brought escalated tension and heightened fears. (There are white kids in black gangs, black kids in Mexican gangs, Mexicans in white gangs, and Asians in everyone's gangs.) It is no longer a race thing. It's who's in the "hood."

"The problem of the twentieth century is the problem of the color line," W. E. B. DuBois wrote in 1903. A century later, we see that although the color line has blurred, the United States, increasingly multicultural, increasingly diverse, is hardly a blended nation. Urban learners cross the line every day.

The annual publication of the U.S. Census Bureau on income and poverty, entitled *Income and Poverty* (1999), reports African Americans continue to experience a significantly disproportionate poverty rate of 23.6 percent. American Indians also suffer from a poverty rate of 25.9 percent. In 1999, we also saw a very high 16.9 percent of the numbers of children living in poverty. This breaks down to over 32 million Americans, including 12 million children, who continue to live in poverty.

We see that the color line, the class line, the culture line, and the gender line have not been erased. Those who have been denied full opportunity in the past are not yet experiencing the good life in the same ratio as their more privileged fellow citizens. Yet there is reason for hope. Many students today attend multicultural, multiethnic schools that mirror the world they will live in as adults.

Improving the quality of public education has emerged as one of the nation's major concerns. And nowhere are these concerns more evident than in America's inner-city schools. Urban schools often face challenges that would daunt other organizations, public or private. Investigations show that although problems of learning in inner cities may seem similar (low academic achievement, higher rates of dropouts, and school violence), the causes and solutions may vary from city to city and among school sites. For example, the flux of immigrant children from Mexico and the various Asian nations into Los Angeles contrasts sharply with the virtually all-black schools in parts of Detroit, Philadelphia, and Chicago.

The litany of hurdles confronting these schools and the children they enroll are now familiar, but the solutions to their problems have only recently emerged from the research. Potential solutions include comprehensive early childhood education, extended time for learning before and after school and during summers, higher academic standards, better teaching and professional development for teachers, adequate facilities, stiffer accountability, and smaller class sizes.

"Giving inner-city children a chance at better education is the best way to break the poverty cycle," says Clint Bolick of the Landmark Center for Civil Rights (Olson and Jerald 1998). "Community support is critical to my urban district's ability to improve its schools."

Are American schools in trouble? Do inner-city students suffer the most? Despite ever-increasing funding for education, test scores have been falling since 1963, and many say it is virtually impossible to get a decent education in an inner-city public school.

Critiques of urban schooling invariably start with the presumption that urban public schools are in a state of crisis and end with clarion calls for more change and new "solutions." These critiques have dominated the discourse and lent urgency to calls for urban reform since *A Nation at Risk* scathingly criticized the nation's schools in 1983. Reform proposals have produced a great deal of activity but little real change in urban education.

Those of us interested in improving the education of children living in urban areas must continue to struggle for a new educational design based on an educational covenant that includes all children regardless of race, class, gender, or disability. A high standard, perhaps, but one worth meeting and exceeding.

3

PASSION FOR TEACHING: ROLE OF THE TEACHERS

To love what you do and feel that it matters, how could anything be more fun?

—Katharine Graham

Today's schools face enormous challenges. In response to an increasingly complex society and a rapidly changing technology-based economy, schools are being asked to educate the most diverse student body in our history to higher academic standards than ever before. This task is one that cannot be "teacher-proofed" through management systems, testing mandates, or curriculum packages. Programs are being designed in which teachers show deep understanding of subject content and are flexible enough to help students create cognitive maps, relate ideas to one another, and address misconceptions. Teachers are connecting ideas across fields and to everyday life. They are teaching in ways that connect with students as well as forming a foundation that includes understanding differences that may arise from culture, family experiences, and learning styles.

Teachers are speaking out for change. This country's public schools employ many talented, committed educators. Unfortunately, these excellent teachers often are frustrated by a system that does not value their skills. They are disappointed by an administrative bureaucracy that sometimes stifles their creativity.

John Dewey (1916) stated that the aim of all good teaching should be to assist each student in reaching his or her fullest potential. For the won't learners, a teacher's instruction must be so powerfully effective that it reaches through to the intelligence and learning capacity that students have despite the crime, poverty, and drugs that pervade their lives.

When asked about the teachers that their children have in alternative and charter schools, the parents interviewed said: "The teachers are great." "They are mentors." "They are innovative, creative, gifted, and patient." "They have an intuitive gift for making each student feel his or her ideas are intelligent, valued, and beneficial."

Teachers report that they are choosing alternative and charter schools to work in because of the philosophy of the school, the smaller class size, and the fact they have more authority and a less stifling bureaucracy. Teachers went on to say that their job is to help individual students to clarify their aspirations, develop plans for the step-by-step attainment of those aspirations, monitor students' progress, and then try to understand and alleviate the problems students encounter. The faculty maintains a climate of high expectations in academic subjects and maintains an interdisciplinary dialogue that helps prevent students from "falling through the cracks."

Strategies of teaching must be grounded in an understanding of students' unique multiple identities and communities. Teaching about and from the cultures of the students is more than a political statement; it is sound educational theory. Students construct knowledge by incorporating new understanding with the background that they bring into the classroom. Knowledge of the characteristics of groups to which students belong, about the importance of each of these groups to the individuals, and of the extent to which the individual has been socialized within each group gives the teacher important clues to students' behavior and attitude.

What makes a teacher good? Looking at the ways we have answered that question in the past century may help.

As many kinds of good teachers are in our schools as varieties of good apples in supermarkets. Unfortunately, we tend to recognize and honor only one kind of teacher at a time. We currently glorify teachers whose students pass standardized tests. In the 1990s, we admired those who had proven they could bring about greater student achievement. In the 1980s, good teachers were those who followed Madeline Hunter's prescription for teaching success. The list goes on and on.

Let's identify some of the visions of good teachers, then begin to explore how we can value these visions, how we can support the development of many kinds of teachers, and how these teachers work with our diverse learners.

For the first half of the twentieth century, school principals, supervisors, and education professors determined the attributes of good teachers. These teachers needed to have such traits as professional attitude, understanding of students, creativity, and demonstrate classroom control, planning skills, and pupil participation. Thus, an *ideal* teacher met subjective standards of excellence determined by selected significant others.

By the early 1960s, administrators encountered problems with measuring attributes of ideal teachers. In a search for some other way to judge teachers, experts soon began describing good teachers as analytic.

Analytic teachers methodically inspected what they did in the classroom. They recorded and examined their classroom practice, how much and about what teachers spoke of, how much and about what students talked about, and the extent and nature of student silence and confusion.

In 1966, the influential Coleman Report asserted that students' socioeconomic backgrounds influenced their learning more than their teachers did. Immediately, dozens of educational researchers set out to show that teachers made a crucial difference in student achievement. These *effective* teachers were found to carefully monitor learning activities; were clear, supportive, and accepting of students; and persistently challenged and engaged them.

Next came *dutiful* teachers, who did not display the typical attributes of effective teachers, such as enthusiasm, but could still bring about student learning. Teachers had to show how well they understood and performed their duties: knowledge of subject matter, school, and community; demonstrated classroom skills, including testing and grading; and provided service to the profession.

The accountability movement in the 1970s spurred an effort to identify *competent* teachers. These teachers had to show competencies in the areas of planning instruction, implementing instruction, assessing and evaluating students, communicating, and performing administrative duties.

In the 1980s and into the 1990s, many scholars used expertise to describe a good teacher. *Expert* teachers had extensive and accessible knowledge that was organized for use in teaching, they were efficient and could do more in less time, and were said to be able to arrive at novel and appropriate solutions to problems.

Another type of teacher that emerged was the *reflective* teacher. They are students of teaching with a strong interest in learning about the art and science of teaching. Reflective teachers are introspective, examining their own practice of teaching by reading scholarly and professional journals and books.

Satisfying teachers please students, parents or caregivers, colleagues, and administrators by responding to their needs. School or parent organizations recognize these teachers by presenting them with awards for good teaching. Admiration shows up by students taking their classes, fellow teachers look to them for guidance, parents want their children in their classes, and administrators trust this teacher to respond positively to difficult students.

We can pinpoint *diversity-responsive* teachers. These instructors take special interest in and are sensitive to students who are different culturally, socially, economically, intellectually, physically, or emotionally. Diversity-responsive teachers are also dedicated to bettering the lives of students both inside and outside the classroom.

Finally, we have *respected* teachers. Real and fictional, respected teachers are often idolized in books and films. Some of the real ones include LouAnne Johnson in *Dangerous Minds*, Jaime Escalante in *Stand and Deliver*, and Marva Collins in *The Marva Collins Story*. Fictional, virtuous teachers have been created in *Mr. Holland's Opus*, *The Prime of Miss Jean Brodie*, *Up the Down Staircase*, *To Sir with Love*, and *Goodbye, Mr. Chips*.

Respected teachers possess and demonstrate qualities including honesty, fairness, devotion, empathy, and selflessness. Most such teachers also have determination, overcoming great odds to ensure student success.

None of these categories is mutually exclusive. No variation, by itself, has proven to be just right. None satisfies all educational stakeholders. In a utopian world, teachers would demonstrate all aspects of teacher "goodness" and possess the attributes of all ten visions (ideal, analytic, effective, dutiful, competent, expert, reflective, satisfying, diversity-responsive, and respected). In the real world, we must accept, recognize, and appreciate many models that teachers can follow.

Sustaining the belief that there are all kinds of good teachers serves several useful ends. First, it dispels the traditional notion that there is only one kind of good teacher. Second, it permits teachers to describe what kind of teacher they are. Third, it provides positive direction for continuing development. We are thus enabled to move forward and to do what is best for the students involved.

Consistently, studies have found that flexibility, adaptability, and creativity are among the most important determinants of teachers' effectiveness. Teaching, more than virtually any activity (aside from parenting), depends on quick, instinctive habits and behavior and on deeply held ways of seeing and valuing. If we want to keep the curriculum and learning opportunities fresh, we have to make it possible for our students to go from outside the subject to inside. Sharing enthusiasm about the subject that is being taught will help develop rapport with students. Tapping into our personal experiences will enhance our teaching worlds. A teacher's interpersonal skills are essential to creating a positive school culture/climate. In other words, good teaching requires an interpersonal repertoire that is both broad and flexible.

The multidimensionality of teaching and the vast array of differences among students are realities that prescriptions for practice cannot account for. Over and over again, teachers stress that the effective teaching that leads to student engagement and learning cannot occur if they cannot connect with students' interests, needs, experiences, and motives. Teachers need to consider the students' interests and stay in tune with what students are thinking and doing. If what a teacher is doing does not coincide with the backgrounds of the students, then the class is lost.

Teachers' insistence on attending to students' experiences, interests, and prior knowledge was once thought to result from a disregard for scientific methods. Now, however, these considerations are supported by cognitive research demonstrating that learning is a process of making meaning out of new or unfamiliar events in light of familiar ideas or experiences. Learners construct knowledge as they build cognitive maps for organizing and interpreting new information. Effective teachers help students make such maps by drawing connections among different concepts and between new ideas and learners' prior experiences. In other words, students learn skills and concepts as tools to meet present demands rather than as facts to be memorized today in hopes of application tomorrow. Teachers must help children learn by allowing them to mobilize their innate capacities to meet everyday challenges that they perceive as meaningful.

One of the qualities that make us fully human and distinguish us from other species is our capacity to invent and discover both knowledge and beauty and to pass our understanding on to successive generations. Every other species begins, in effect, at Darwinian ground zero with respect to their predecessors. Offspring may be little different from what their ancestors were ten generations ago, but different for evolutionary reasons, not because the previous generation carefully nurtured, nourished, preserved, and transformed information and then passed it on. Teachers are one mechanism by which our societies pass on knowledge and values. Teachers, in that sense, are uniquely responsible for carrying on our cultural, intellectual, and aesthetic achievements.

Again the question: What makes a good teacher? Richard P. Traina, president of Clark University in Worcester, Massachusetts, embarked on an interesting bit of research in pursuit of an answer to just that query. He explored 125 autobiographies of prominent Americans from the nineteenth and twentieth centuries. As these men and women of different social, economic, geographic, religious, and racial backgrounds recounted their educational experiences, three descriptions came to light over and over again: competence in the subject matter, caring deeply about the students and their successes, and the teachers' distinctive characters.

A command of the subject matter, such that the students pick up on the teacher's excitement about it, is fundamental. For example, Phil's incredible knowledge of tropical fish found in his tanks at his apartment or his description of what his snake ate for dinner is meaningful to the students, especially since his students have been taken to his apartment to view the tanks and the snake. Bruce's leading questions about social issues are opening the student's mind up for learning, making the students more engaged. Both teachers are allowing their students to see the world differently.

A second characteristic is equally important: caring deeply about the student's accomplishments and growth. The teacher recognizes the student as an individual who brings particular experience, interests, enthusiasm, and fears into the classroom. When the teacher takes time to acknowledge a student's life outside the classroom, relationships develop.

When teachers visit the neighborhood organizations that their students attend, they can begin to build connections between community organizations and the classroom. For instance, a high school English teacher in California saw one of her low-achieving students in an entirely new light when she watched him star in a play produced by a youth group. In Pennsylvania, an English teacher who visited a church-based literacy project saw his students researching and writing for the church newsletter in ways he had not seen in his classroom, and he revised his writing curriculum to make the most of their after-school experience. A school in southern California provides teachers with professional development time to visit churches, athletic programs, and youth clubs in the neighborhoods their students reside in. These teachers now view neighborhood youth organizations as valuable learning resources. They care deeply about their students and there is an insistence that the students take pride in their work, stretching their minds to a level of performance that excites everyone involved.

The third attribute, distinctive character, is the most elusive; it gives flavor or texture to the other two. In almost all cases, there is something distinctive about the character of the teacher recalled by the student. Joel, whose military career included submarine operation, and Marcus, a gentle elementary teacher who is an ex-pro football player, have experiences that lend themselves to exciting stories and respect. A palpable energy suffices the competent and caring teacher as mark-making quality.

The combination of these three attributes is extremely powerful. Students believe that their teachers are changing their lives. It should not be surprising that a vital bond through all levels of education is a competent, caring, character-inspired teacher.

Teachers have developed certain characteristics that are necessary for effectively teaching won't learners and all students.

- A teacher must have high expectations.
- A teacher should show intense personal warmth in combination with a demand for a high level of achievement expressed as personal concern for the student.
- A teacher should use democratic practices in the classroom so that the students and teacher are united in planning, organizing, implementing, and participating in their common activities.
- A teacher should use a combination of firmness and kindness, indirect criticism, joshing, and joking.
- A teacher is a model who sets the stage for learning, acceptance, and respect.

Now let's dialogue with some of these teachers. The teachers interviewed had the following comments about working with our won't learners. These interviews were conducted between January and July 2001.

Won't learners have a great need for intimacy, yet we place them in large, impersonal schools. They need increased autonomy and the right to make their own decisions, yet we put them in environments of review and rote learning. There is a great variability among them and within themselves, yet we put them in classrooms where we ignore their variability and need for flexibility. My alternative school focuses equally on the characteristics and needs of young people. The school is a community of adults and youth embedded in networks of support and responsibility that enhance learning. (Indian male, thirteen years of teaching)

I believe that the best features of schools that help kids are active, in-depth learning, appreciation of diversity, collaborative learning, a great support system, and connections to the family and the community. (White female, fifteen years teaching in special education)

The won't learner must be actively engaged in inquiring about and constructing his or her own meaning if learning is to take place. (Hispanic male, ten years of teaching)

We teach social and emotional learning. The kids that we are dealing with are disadvantaged and do not know how to thrive or survive in a traditional school. They put up walls and "won't learn." They do not have the hopes and dreams that inspire academic success. We can no longer ignore out-of-school lives. My school is an integral part of the lives of the families and the students. (African American male, eight years of teaching)

I spent thirty-one years of teaching in a large, impersonal school system and never once could do my own thing to motivate kids. Even in my coaching, I had my hands tied by the powers that reside above. Now I can teach kids who need me, team teach, do flexible scheduling, and share in the management of the school. (White male, thirty-three years of teaching)

Let the students speak. Students interviewed said that one of the primary reasons for choosing a school were the teachers in the program.

A good teacher tells me what is out there to learn, shows an enthusiasm for acquiring knowledge for the purpose of understanding, and then turns me loose to learn at my own pace.

The teachers are boss! They really care. They are sensitive to who I am and they respect me. They are part of my life. They are great.

We like the good teachers who teach until we get it. They won't let me fall behind or fail. They make an effort to understand me.

You are more than just a teacher and principal. You are a friend and someone who is always there for me. I trust you and you make me feel important. You make me feel my mistakes are simply learning experiences. You believe in me.

We were both going to drop out of school until we met you. You cared for us and made us feel like we were someone. You never doubted that we could make it. You loved us.

All of the teachers interviewed said they chose to work in alternative settings or charter schools because they were allowed to focus on the students. Our won't learners have experienced disproportional school failure in educational systems organized, administered, and controlled by a bureaucracy that believes in "one size fits all." Research has found that students who maintain a strong sense of pride in their own culture and who have not internalized mixed feelings about that culture tend not to experience school failure. Many of the learning difficulties of our won't learners are often caused by the way we teach children designated "at-risk." These students frequently receive intensive instruction that confines them to a passive role and induces a form of "learned helplessness." A model that allows for reciprocal interactions between teacher and student (that focuses on the student) represents the best alternative for won't learners. Alternative schools and charter schools are set up to focus on the individual student and to provide for educational opportunities to help children who have not succeeded in existing schools.

The teachers interviewed said that the won't learners need to see morals, values, and skills modeled. They believe teachers who communicate core values in their everyday work and reinforce values in their actions and words help sculpt the school climate for won't learners. By listening to students responsively, we convey the message that they matter. We listen and are nonjudgmental.

Teachers who demonstrate competency and interest in their subject area as well as additional areas will help our won't learners become accountable, competent, and interested. We feel especially successful when we see a frustrated child begin to relax and enjoy learning. Teachers can convey the paradigm that learning is reflective and active, verbal and nonverbal, concrete and abstract, and involves head and heart. Our teachers are empowered, listened to, and personalize for the learners. By paying attention to the varied learning styles of all our students, we can do more to accomplish the goals of education.

Won't learners are constantly monitoring the adults around them. In the area of ethical values, teachers must be cognizant of how their words and actions coincide with the values they profess to uphold. Developing the mind and hands is education; developing the hands alone is mere training.

The teachers also stated that one thing that makes a difference to won't learners is respect. If you do not respect the people you teach and you do not have a feeling that the learners are of equal value to yourself, that they can become who and what they choose, then you will not teach much to your students. Teachers must model courage, truth, humility, wisdom, love, respect, and honesty, and must connect these values to the school setting.

The teachers interviewed also feel support for the learners; the trust issue becomes an important component in their teaching styles. Teaching is the art of leading our learners to realize their potential. When we support our young people, we support ourselves. Never quit. Go the distance. Teachers must believe in their students even when they appear to be failing, disruptive, suspended, or thrown out. Teachers must believe in their students even when the students do not believe in themselves. This is part of establishing trust.

Building trust is a complex task to achieve when working with our won't learners. Establishing trust and cooperation are essential components for teachers if they are to understand the relationship between home, poor school adjustment, and underachievement of the won't learners. These interviewed teachers say: "Caring is crucial to the development of young men and women in turning them into healthy adults. They need to see themselves as valued members of a group that offers mutual support and trust." "Schools should be a place where close, trusting relationships with adults and other students create a climate for personal growth and intellectual development." "Trust is essential for all kids. The students trust us and we trust them."

What motivates teachers to work with won't learners, or any learners for that matter? Student success, student achievement, student enthusiasm, and seeing children learn are just a small part of it. Teachable moments in the streets, the parks, and the homes say it all. Teachers want to satisfy the unmet needs of the children they serve. These teachers believe

- Learners need to be cast in an active role within the school.
- Learners are to be encouraged to create and recreate knowledge for themselves.
- We must offer options, resources, and guidance and then participate, model, and demonstrate.
- We must recognize the value of the student as thinker.
- We must recognize that children are different; when we respect this individuality and listen to what they say, instruction will become clearer.
- We must respect and appreciate the different cultures and move to accept, validate, and acknowledge the experiences, languages, and traditions of our diverse students.
- What children learn is as important as how they learn.
- We are facilitators, coaches, and guides.

The teachers also say that they

- Are caring and supportive
- Advocate positive expectations
- Maintain a climate of high expectations in academic subjects
- Believe that behavior and attitudes convey a message that "You can do it" and "I won't give up on you"
- Personalize for their students
- Are empowered
- Use "teachable moments"
- Share enthusiasm

Teachers at many alternative and charter schools who work with the won't learners

- Place relationships before rules
- Use "outside the box" thinking
- Share ownership and decision making
- Understand the importance of emotions and feelings as critical to effective learning and teaching
- View all students as winners
- Use cooperative learning techniques and group work to promote racial and ethnic integration of the school and the classroom
- Are in touch with their own cultural and ethnic knowledge (By understanding our own racial identity, we are able to support the positive development of our students' racial and ethnic identities.)

The teachers interviewed said that the old one-size-fits-all approach allows too many learners to fall through the cracks. These students are intelligent but continue to struggle in school. We must therefore structure opportunities into each learner's daily routine that will enable him or her to experience feelings of competence (evidence of test scores, academic success), belonging (valued members of the school), usefulness (made a contribution through service learning and cooperative learning), potency (feeling empowered, goal setting), and optimism (I can do it).

One key for getting students to relate to the environment is when teachers give students a voice in the classroom. Students need to become decision makers, to act as teachers, to reflect on mistakes, and to gain empowerment through responsibility.

If we want to nurture students who will grow into lifelong learners, into self-directed seekers, into the kinds of adults who are morally responsible even when someone else is not looking, then we need to find our students opportunities to practice making choices and reflecting on the outcomes.

If we are to reach our won't learners, teachers must continue to establish high standards, provide all students with challenging coursework, and support their need to reach these standards. Teachers must be empowered to organize their schools into personal communities and then create incentives for the learners to study and achieve.

As teachers, we can honor our students' search for what they believe gives meaning and integrity to their lives, and how they can connect to what is most precious for them. We can allow students the freedom to choose what to study and have a say in how they might prove to their teacher that they are making progress. How the content is taught is equally as important as the content itself when we determine student mastery. We simply help the learner discover that knowledge contributes to power, friendship, and fun.

School is where the children are making teachers the role models. Sociologists have long argued that learning is transmitted from generation to generation through role models.

Tedious, coercive schooling creates frustrations that emerge sooner or later in self-depreciation, despair, or violence against others. However, where a real connection is made between students and teachers in the pursuit of meaningful accomplishments, the possibilities for developing lifelong capacities for learning, doing, and relating to others are greatly expanded.

Many teachers are proud of their students, so enamored with learning, so happy to be there. Listen to a teacher talk about his or her charges as they demonstrate an understanding of their students' personal as well as intellectual needs. They also know the value of hooking the students, of making the subjects real, of giving kids a reason to learn. Don't let your students ask, "Why do I have to learn this?" Make everything that they learn relate to the real world. Teachers should become folks with a mission of which the child is a part. Let your classroom make learning come alive. Reinforce learning across disciplines, celebrate diversity, and inculcate democratic values and you will create an environment that is appealing to learners.

In 1916, John Dewey defined teaching as the capacity to look at things as if they could be different. In June 1999, Maxine Green extended that definition during a speech at UCLA: "If you say what might be, then you make intolerable what is. How, then, can we help teachers see how schools, classrooms, teaching, and learning could be different?"

Teachers, ask yourselves and each other these three questions:

1. Am I treating the students with dignity and respect?
2. Were the objectives of the lesson worthwhile and challenging?
3. To what extent did the students achieve and learn?

Reflecting on these questions captures the three crucial aspects of teaching: intent, process, and outcome. Answering these questions positively leads to learner success. Always remember that who you teach should shape how you teach because who the students are shapes how they learn.

Learning is possible when children look hopefully and joyfully to the future. Unless we project hope for our students, our efforts to teach them to read, write, and calculate won't make a profound difference. A teacher's task is not only to engage students' imagination but also to convince our students that they are people of worth who can do something in a very different world. When children lack resources, it is very easy to give up on hope.

Teachers nurture the moral and spiritual development, the civic engagement, and the socialization of students, a nurturing we usually associate with parents, clergy, social workers, librarians, and all the people who jointly accept the responsibility for both raising and protecting the young. Teachers, in particular, play a singular role in our society in nurturing students.

4

DISTRUST OF THE SYSTEM: ROLE OF THE PARENTS

There can be hope only for a society which acts as one big family, and not as many separate ones.

—Anwar al-Sadat

Cesar works the assembly line at the Coke plant southeast of Minneapolis, Minnesota. Everyday he is at work by 6:30 A.M., and he often works seven days a week. After he returns home, he practices reading and writing in English with his children before heading to his evening English as a second language (ESL) class at a nearby community center. Cesar's education in the countryside of El Salvador was interrupted after only five years by civil war and the need to help support his family. Despite these obstacles, Cesar is learning English alongside his children.

Ilham is a housekeeper in a downtown Minneapolis hotel. Although the Iraqi immigrant is tired when she returns home in late afternoon, she looks over her son's homework and, if she has the energy, she speaks to him in her native Kurdish, a language he does not understand as well as English. Ilham's job is taxing and her English class is difficult because, unlike most of her classmates, Ilham is not accustomed to the Roman alphabet. She is very optimistic about her son's prospects. "For myself, I don't care; I want to help my son for the future. I want him to go to college."

Daysi cooks for a tiny bar in northeast Minneapolis. She leaves for work at 3:00 P.M. after her oldest daughter arrives home from high school to baby-sit five younger siblings. Closing at the bar can be any-time from 1:00 A.M. to 4:00 A.M. and she goes immediately to bed on ar-rival home. Her daughter is responsible for getting the younger children into bed, up in the morning, and off to school. Daysi is trying to get into computer class so she can become a secretary and work normal hours.

Homer is a retired grandfather of fifteen who recently acquired two teenagers when his middle daughter was killed in a drive-by shooting. He is starting parenting again. Homer is utilizing support from Grand-parents as Parents, an agency within Volunteers of America that net-works with grandparents who have found themselves in the role of par-ents once again.

These parents exemplify the qualities that we seek to instill in our children. They are hardworking, persistent, ambitious, compassionate, and they value education. Yet these parents often work long or irregular hours, sometimes holding down two jobs, and may have limited English proficiency.

Although the above parents may value education, we must also face the fact that many of the parents we are dealing with feel the opposite. These are the parents who have had bad experiences in school them-selves and equally bad experiences with their children's schools today.

Only a quarter of America's households fit the old *Leave It to Beaver* model, and single mothers are on the front lines, raising kids and re-defining the meaning of "family." Today's moms may be divorced or never married, rich or poor, living with men or on their own. With tra-ditional households in decline, they are the new faces in the school fam-ily album.

Just imagine what would happen if June and Ward Cleaver, parents of the Beaver, were negotiating family life these days. The scenario might go something like this: They meet at the office or a bar and move in to-gether after dating for a couple of months. A year later, June gets preg-nant. What to do? Neither feels ready to make it legal and there is no pressure from their parents, all of whom are divorced and remarried themselves. So little Wally is welcomed into the world with June's last name on the birth certificate. A few years later, June gets pregnant again. The Beaver is born and Ward is ambivalent about second-time fa-therhood and moves out. June decides to go ahead on her own. In her neighborhood, single motherhood is no big deal; the lesbians down the street adopted kids from South America and the soccer mom next door is divorced with a live-in boyfriend.

Figures from the 2000 census show that this postmodern June would be almost as mainstream as the 1950s version. The number of families headed by single mothers has increased 25 percent since 1990, to more than 7.5 million households. Contributing to the numbers are high rates of divorce and out-of-wedlock births. A third of all babies were born to unmarried women, compared with 3.8 percent in 1940. More than half of the children born in the 1990s spent at least a part of their childhood in a single-parent home. The number of single fathers raising kids on their own is now over 2 million. Married couples, raising children, account for less than a quarter of all households (U.S. Census Bureau 2000).

Demographers and politicians will likely spend years arguing about what all this means and whether the shifts are real or just numerical flukes. The one thing everyone does agree on is that single mothers are now a permanent and significant page in America's diverse family album.

Single mothers have less time for each individual child than two parents, and cohabiting relationships are less stable than marriages. That means that children living in these families are more likely to grow up with a revolving set of adults in their lives. The offspring of single parents are more likely to skip the altar themselves, thus perpetuating the pattern of their childhood. "Children living outside marriage are seven times more likely to end up on welfare and to have a propensity for emotional problems, discipline problems, early pregnancy, and abuse," says Robert Rector, a senior research fellow at the Heritage Foundation, a conservative think tank (Public Agenda Report 2000).

What does this mean for the schools?

The tension between families and the schools they are involved with is increasing partly because children in general are not doing well in our country. This is especially true of our teenagers in terms of their intellectual, social, emotional, and moral development. Parents and teachers appear to be lost, confused, and scared, so are often yelling at one another. There is distrust in all institutions, much of which started during the Vietnam crisis and has not been helped by America's war on terror, striking back abroad, counterstrikes and scares, biochemical warfare, national security issues, foreign policy, and our roller coaster economy. We have issues with authority. Our values have changed. The things parents in the early part of the twentieth century most wanted from their children were compliance and cooperation. It is just the opposite now: parents want their children to be independent, to question policies, and to form their own perspectives.

We also have a culture of narcissism. Advertisements and popular psychology create confusion about what we want from children. Schools are confused about accountability. Across the country, a single idea has become the new buzzword in educational reform: "accountability." What does this buzzword mean? Is accountability as generic as improving student performance? Or does it involve curriculum, goals and objectives, improved attendance, lower dropout rates, or financial planning? When a school promises to take certain steps that will result in improved conditions, the school must make good on its promise. Accountability is a matter of taking responsibility for the content and process of goals set, decisions made, actions taken, and outcomes that result from them. It is about making agreements and engaging in activities with the full expectation that they will be carried out in the most competent, high-quality, conscientious manner possible. The confusion arises when parents want attention to their children's needs and the schools do not provide the appropriate response. Accountability must be a motivating force that guides daily practice within a school.

For every child living in poverty, there are one or more adult parents living in poverty as well (U.S. Census Bureau 2000). Poverty places much the same stress on adults as it does on children and adolescents. It sharply increases the odds of violence, family instability, and a variety of self-destructive behaviors such as smoking, drug and alcohol addiction, and risky sexual conduct that influences the next generation. Educators can hardly be expected to remedy the educational and economic disparities of the families they serve. Educators should, however, be aware of how they respond to parents and students from a multitude of different backgrounds. Culture lies in values and practices, not in ethnic labels.

Parents need to be brought into the educational community whenever possible. Cooperation and support from parents can lead to a positive climate in the classroom. Orderliness depends on constant communication among teachers, students, and parents. School performance often affects how students relate and communicate with parents.

The process of bringing parents together, talking, listening, developing a shared vision, and creating a plan of action has value in and of itself. It brings parents into conversation and decision making. It builds trust and good will.

A parent as a partner in classrooms and schools is hardly a novel concept, but implementing the idea is far from easy. Public agenda surveys tell us that parents and educators do not see eye to eye, and that while parents do not necessarily agree with one another about what good teaching is, they are increasingly skeptical of what the experts say it is. Experts often define good teaching as knowing the subject matter, having classroom discipline, or using Madeline Hunter's model for lesson plans. Parents may feel that caring, trust, knowledge of cultural diversity, and communication are the answers to good teaching. Misunderstandings are rife, and efforts to reform schools are stifled when, in fact, improved education is what most parents want.

Schools cannot meet the challenges of reform without first communicating with the parents. You will find that parents want authenticity. In a revealing series of research studies conducted in 1987, Jane Lindle found that while educators thought parents expected them to be "professional and businesslike," parents and guardians actually wanted the opposite. Parents at all socioeconomic levels complained about teachers and principals being "patronizing" and "talking down to us." They wanted educators to be real in 1987 and want the same today.

Although public engagement requires planning and energy, it depends not so much on organizational design as on attitude and personal characteristics. It takes honesty and humility, patience and kindness, openness and empathy. It takes authenticity.

The parents of our won't learners will speak out forcefully if given the chance. When asked what they really want from schools, the parents interviewed said

- A curriculum that promotes cultural competence and appreciates ethnic diversity
- Instructional methods that promote cooperation, interaction, and success for all students
- Assessment practices that include alternative methods that allow for cultural differences and encourage community review
- Public conversation that is sensitive to the perception and values of the total community

What do parents want from teachers?

There have been three consistent parental concerns identified: how well teachers know and care about teaching, about their children, and about communicating with parents.

Here is what they say about teaching: Teachers need to smile, often. Teachers need to share stories, not only about interests and successes but also about funny things that happen in school. A good laugh together between parents and teachers is a strong bond.

Teachers need to sit and share with parents their high expectations and specific learning goals for the children. Parents also want teachers to share academics, explaining the curriculum, their teaching methods, and how parents can reinforce learning at home. Parents want to see the classroom in action.

Parents have this to say about their children: "We want teachers to know our children, to identify their abilities and build on them, to show respect." Parents want to be notified when issues arise. Parents also want to be called when their child deserves praise.

Parents had this to say about communication: "We want the teachers to be accessible, responsive, and cooperative." They also want to hear and see a familiar, positive portrait of their child. The communication should include shared values. In our increasingly diverse world, finding common ground is essential.

"I knew right from the start that I was in sync with my daughter's eighth grade social studies teacher," commented one parent. "The teacher spoke further of expectations for all students. He spoke of kindness, responsibility, and effort. He was speaking my language." No one will argue with the virtues of fairness, honest effort, and hard work. When a child's performance is critiqued, the conversation should be about effort, discipline, responsibility, standards, and integrity.

Parents have a tough job raising children in today's world. In a 1997 Public Agenda Report, four out of five Americans say that it is much harder for parents to do their job these days. The mothers and fathers of our students are aware of the increased demands on their time and the stresses in their lives. Factor in fears about violence, date rape, and AIDS, and you can understand parental nightmares. A little empathy with parents' predicaments can go a long way in establishing a bond of trust.

Consider the following open letter from a parent:

I am your worst nightmare. I am the parent who will make phone calls, write letters, and be at your door if I think your great new educational idea is nothing more than reform du jour. You and I see change from different perspectives. I have a very narrow set of interests. I do not care about the latest advances in brain research. I won't get excited about claims of potential big performance gains. If you tell me about self-esteem one more time, I will become ill. Although I want what is best for all students, I am much more interested in how your proposal will affect my child. I have a special responsibility to him or her. I will not let you forget his or her needs so you can help someone else. If you want my support, talk to me specifically about your reform's impact on my child. After you address my child's needs, I will think about the potential benefits to others.

Parents are trusting schools with the well-being of their children. The schools must take that responsibility seriously. If educators show parents that they honestly care about the children, parents will be more inclined to place faith in the educational system and accept its role in the life of their child.

One parent said: "I do not wish to sacrifice my child on the altar of the future. Talk to me about today."

Another showed her feelings: "I truly believe my son will be more successful and well-rounded in life by learning in an environment that is diverse in culture and academically challenging."

In many school districts across the country, parents are allowed to choose, for their children, any public school within their district that has openings. Many communities have "choice" schools, or schools which specialize in a particular discipline (multiple intelligences, the arts, or math and science). These schools can be schools within a school, magnet schools, alternative schools, or public charter schools.

In many states, the Open Enrollment Statute allows parents to have the option of enrolling their children in another district through "exception to attendance" procedures. Home schooling is an additional option. But simply choosing a school does not empower parents to be full participants in their child's education.

Only when parents are given sufficient information to make informed choices, when all students are provided free transportation, when the selection process for entry into chosen programs is fair and open, when all schools meet the same minimum educational standards and adhere to state and national regulations, when all schools are held publicly accountable, and when money is not diverted from public education budgets, only then will all children have an opportunity for a quality public education.

Many parents do not realize that the educational world has changed dramatically since they were in school. Several years ago, schools were smaller, class sizes were smaller, dropout rates were lower, and violence in school was at a minimum. Even through rose-colored glasses, we knew that school was no picnic and was far from perfect. Because our public school system has deteriorated, many parents, teachers, and individuals have taken it upon themselves to find alternatives to the traditional system. It is important for parents to know that they now have alternatives to the neighborhood school.

How do parents know it is time to look for another educational approach for their child? Here are some of the signs:

- Does your child hate school? If so, something is probably wrong with the school. Children are natural learners; if your child says he hates school, listen.
- Does your child come home from school bored and cranky? This is a sign that her educational experiences are not energizing but are actually debilitating.
- Does your child come home complaining about conflicts he has had in school or talking about unfair situations he has been exposed to? This is a sign that the school does not have a proper process for conflict resolution and communication is lacking.
- Has your child stopped reading for fun, or writing for pleasure? This is a sign that these activities are not being valued in the school. She is losing creativity.
- Does your child refuse to do homework? This may be a sign that the homework is not interesting, does not meet his needs, and is tending to extinguish natural curiosity.
- Does your child come home talking about anything exciting that happened in school that day? If not, maybe nothing exciting is tak-

ing place. Would you want to keep working if your job was like that?

- Did the school nurse or guidance counselor suggest that your child has some strange three-lettered disease, like ADD? Have you been told your child needs Ritalin or some other drug? It may be more probable that the school has the disease EDD (Education Deficit Disorder). It is time to remove your child from that situation.

If children have exhibited several of the above characteristics, it is time to start looking for an alternative. Check out charter schools, magnet schools, Montessori schools, Waldorf schools, and alternative schools.

As more and more parents become aware of these choices, the system may evolve into one that meets the needs of an increasing number of students. Don't wait for the system to change. Take responsibility for the children.

School choice is the hottest and most controversial idea in educational reform today. As dissatisfaction with the public schools continues to grow, more and more people are turning to choice to provide real reform.

Parents are enthusiastic about the alternative schools their children attend. One mother said, "My son's school presents a fantastic opportunity for kids who have been unsuccessful in traditional schools. We have none of the problems of other schools. It is a safe, caring, loving, secure environment. My son is learning!"

Another parent said, "Individualized learning means you really put my child first. You start her with what she knows and then move forward."

A third parent said: "My son gets all the encouragement and attention he needs in a small innovative school setting. He is no longer just a number in the school's computer."

Parents are speaking out. The parents and families that were interviewed have a multitude of reasons why they are choosing alternative education or particular schools for their children. The two major reasons cited were curriculum and the teachers in the program. Parents want the core essentials of the basics (reading, writing, mathematics, and reasoning), along with a curriculum that emphasizes active participation in meaningful, culturally relevant activities that grow from individual needs and interest.

One parent said, "Make the curriculum relevant and engaging and you will have successful learners."

More and more parents are looking at the teachers in the program. A positive working relationship between teachers and parents is essential for maximum student learning.

One African American parent said, "Too many teachers in traditional schools seem to see their role as rescuer. My child does not need to be rescued. He does not consider being black a misfortune. The teachers here respect him for who he is."

Parents are looking for small classes that permit more personal interaction between teachers and students. "My son thrives in a small class. He gets attention when he needs it, speaks out, and isn't afraid of being laughed at."

More parents are looking at the philosophy of the school. Education should empower students and help each individual to his or her fullest potential. In fact, some parents will go so far as to say that the social, racial, and ethnic characteristics of a school's philosophy may be more important than the curriculum. These parents are looking for a school that will empower their children to become self-directed and active learners.

Individualized learning was also cited as a reason for choosing a school. Unfortunately, many schools seem to take pride in teaching all students the same way. Teachers believe that doing so promotes equality. However, a child's interests, learning style, and developmental level may differ dramatically from his or her peers. What better way to capture the minds of young people than to enroll them in schools they want to attend, tailored to their particular interests. "Individualizing" means that we personalize education by connecting the student's life to the academics in the classroom. When we allow children to make their own educational choices, a learner becomes more highly motivated, satisfied, fulfilled, and successful.

Many of the families interviewed listed parent involvement as a reason for choosing their school. The best way to meet a child's needs is to support and build on the strength of their families. The more parents are involved, the stronger the program will be and the more likely children will succeed in school.

Parents also report that the administrator of the program is a primary factor in school choice. Families gravitate to a person they can trust. Administrators are often the keys to shaping school culture by communicating core values in their everyday work.

A satisfied parent said, "We trust you. You make us feel that this is our school. You care. You are there for us outside of the school. You make us feel like we are somebody important."

Many parents are looking for an extra support system, higher standards of behavior as well as academics, and a hands-on learning environment. Finally, safety and a safe learning environment are reported as being necessary components of parent choice schools. Americans have become so accustomed to stories of horrific violence in schools in the United States that anything short of murder is barely noticed. Studies show that the United States leads the developed world when it comes to violence among school-age children and is the world leader in teenage suicide. Parents want their children in schools where violence and drugs are not serious problems. The key to preventing violence lies in shaping children's beliefs, attitudes, and behaviors before violence becomes an automatic manifestation of their anger.

A concerned parent said, "Kids are coming to school more frightened and angry than ever before and they bring this inside. I've found a school that is promoting cooperation, conflict resolution, and civic values, which combine to make my school a safe haven for kids."

All in all, parents want quality education and attention to their children's needs. When concerns are raised, parents deserve constructive responses; when responses are lacking, they want access to decision makers who are able to address their concerns.

Teachers emphasize that parent involvement is an important piece in the education of won't learners. A student's school performance increases when the parents and extended family are involved in the operation of their child's school. When educators involve the parents as partners in the child's education, the parents appear to communicate a positive attitude toward that education. This leads to involvement in the academic achievement of the student. Teachers operating at the collaborative end of the continuum actively encourage parents to participate in promoting their child's academic progress both in the home and through involvement in classroom activities. Parents allow the teachers to tap their skills, talents, and energy.

How, then, can teachers and administrators reach out to this new breed of parents and involve them in their child's education and in the life of the school? Parent programs should be designed to

- Address parents' individual needs rather than the generic needs assumed by the program developers
- Use a framework that values and promotes cultural diversity
- Increase parent participation
- Highlight communication

The following tips for communicating with parents have proven successful:

- If parents work, call them where they are likely to be reached.
- Schedule parent-teacher conferences on parents' days off (this may mean weekends).
- Send weekly letters home describing what their child did in school. Ask the child to read the letters to their parents, and then talk about what they are learning.
- Encourage parent involvement by elaborating on their child's progress and what they need to practice at home.
- Home visits. Go to the parents.
- Offer family nights with food and include free transportation and babysitting services.

At many alternative schools, family nights are offered three or four times a year. Parents are introduced to the school program and to teachers' expectations. Parents can find out what their children are doing in school and become familiar with routines at home that will help their child succeed. Refreshments are served; in an informal setting, the teachers are available to answer questions. Parents are encouraged to commit to spending time in their child's classroom if at all possible. The message is loud and clear. Parents are welcome in the building at any time.

What do the children have to say in all this? What do children want from their parents?

Parents do not always know what their children think. In her book *Ask the Children* (1999), Ellen Galinsky asked children and parents what response would be given to the question, "If you could change the way that your mother's or father's work affects your life, what would you wish to change?" Most parents guessed that their children would wish for more time with them. Surprisingly, more time was not at the top of the list. Most children wished that their parents would be less stressed, less tired, and less angry. The parents never had a clue. Parental stress affects student stress.

Older children do not give their parents very high marks for knowing what goes on in their lives. Teachers can help parents with communication skills (ask specific questions rather than general ones, appear interested, and listen). Kids want parents to care.

At a recent forum for teens, the participants said that although most of them were good kids, some teens do have a variety of problems. One student put it well: "If we are the problem, then we need to be part of the solution."

Schools have the unique opportunity to harness a parent-student partnership and include both in addressing the different issues that they face. By encouraging open communication, schools, parents, and students become part of the solution.

From advisor to equal partner, from passive listener to decision maker, from fund-raiser to hell-raiser, the role of parents in schools is changing. Schools can no longer view parents as appendages to education or meddlers in school policy.

When schools encourage parents to get involved, grades improve, test scores and graduation rates rise, absenteeism falls, and expectations for students soar. The achievement gains are greatest for those students who start farthest behind. "The research is very clear. When parents are involved, their kids do better in school and the schools get better," says Anne Henderson, an educational policy consultant in Washington, D.C. (Norton 2000). Schools that have an active, engaged parent community feel accountable to that community. They are going to do more, exert more effort, and have higher expectations for their students.

Parental involvement has been proven through years of research to be the most consistent means of improving education in our schools. Parental involvement can and does take many forms in schools and districts across this country. Across the United States, we have parents involved on site teams, on advisory boards, in the classrooms, and in PTAs. The amount of involvement varies greatly, but parental satisfaction in the education their children receive seems to increase. Parents feel empowered.

We all agree that it is important that children have a place to be children. Education is about teaching our children to find pleasure in the right things. Children need adults to care for them in addition to their parents. They need somebody at school who knows them well. Parents also need a personal relationship with the school. The more programs you can open to parents, the more you acknowledge community for all involved.

Inviting parents to volunteer their time increases their sense of ownership and commitment and creates true advocates. Gaining support from parents takes time. Taking steps to involve parents and address their concerns is essential. Once parents see how well their children are doing and how much they enjoy school, parents become partners in the learning process and are the school's biggest supporters.

5

WHERE DO WE BEGIN? HOW DO WE JOURNEY TOGETHER?

Struggle precedes growth.

—Don Coyhis

Pokémon, Beanie Babies, Back Street Boys, Harry Potter, Leonardo di Caprio, Britney Spears, and *Dawson's Creek*. I like getting a dose of what interests young people. Some of the things that may become the cultural artifacts of their times appeal to me; some of them do not. Some of the television shows that I consider exploitative, the won't learners see as authentic depictions of the way they are or want to be.

Every generation remakes itself. No group has a corner on wisdom or silliness. It is a mistake to think that the younger generation wants us to abandon "adult culture" and take up their culture. Young people want to have a culture of their own, and just like to shock us with their body piercing, green hair, and outlandish language.

The won't learners are more immersed in technology than those of us who didn't grow up with it, more skilled and more blasé. They are savvy consumers but, sometimes, slavish materialists. They are alone much of the time; some like it, but many of them are lonely. They want their own identity but they want their teachers to know them and their peers to like them.

It is no secret that the U.S. public school system is in trouble. Students are dropping out at increasingly higher rates each year, many students who do graduate are still functionally illiterate, and the number of students who have diagnosed learning problems requiring special education services is growing. The results are clear: The United States is "dumbing down" as we allow our children to grow up without the ability to read, analyze, and interpret information. The U.S. National Commission on Adult Literacy reported in 1996 that "Ninety million Americans cannot read and write acceptably enough to fix a credit card problem, perform such basic tasks as calculating the difference in price between two items, completing a social security form, or read a bus schedule."

Historically, America's public education system has been a monopolistic franchise. Its "product" is children who can read and write well enough to be contributing members of a democratic society. There is no true competition so there are no rewards for teachers or schools who are successful in teaching students. Conversely, there is no accountability for producing 90 million Americans who are functionally illiterate. No corporation would continue to do business in America with that rate of inferior product.

These trends paint a bleak picture for American educators. If certain things do not change, the cycle of illiteracy will remain constant in our society. Therefore, there is a need for new creative educational models, an opportunity for a truly competitive market, and an accountability for producing children functionally literate and prepared to make informal choices in a democratic society. Recent school reform in America has tackled these issues by experimenting with alternative schools, magnet schools, and charter schools.

Public schools are both the victims and the perpetrators. Our society sends millions of children into the classroom each day who are not equipped to learn. Many are hungry, exhausted, highly stressed, and emotionally vulnerable due to poverty and family problems. These problems facing today's children, youth, and families stem from a variety of economical, political, and social pressures.

Cities are complex ecosystems. The economic, political, and ecological climate of the city bears upon education. It influences the motivation of students and their beliefs concerning the future.

Creativity, clear vision, and realism are necessary as we seek to improve the depleted and unhealthy environment affecting the lives and education of children and youth in inner cities. A knowledge and understanding of city life can form a basis for improving cities' capacity for education.

A basic premise is the desirability of finding what is positive, even in the face of adversity. Focus on the "positives" of inner-city life, the vast resources of the cities, and most importantly, the resilience and potential of inner-city children and youth.

We can begin by promoting educationally resilience in our students. Resilient individuals are characterized in the literature as being proactively engaged in a variety of activities; having well-developed "self-systems"; and able to plan, change their environment, and alter their life circumstances in successful ways. The resilient child is also good at solving problems, having interpersonal skills, and holding to a clear sense of purpose.

Inner-city schools that are effective in promoting educational resilience have the following characteristics:

- Students spent more time working independently.
- Teachers spent more time interacting with students.
- Teachers and students both expressed more positive perceptions about the school.
- Parents are involved and held higher expectations for their children.
- Higher expectations are stressed in all content and behavioral areas.
- The schools held to higher aspirations and encouraged achievement motivation.
- Students had better social and academic self-concepts.
- Teachers are more involved in the school and more supportive of school policy.
- The rules are clear.

As we move forward, it seems logical to expect that inner-city schools would provide a place of refuge and hope for children. Schools provide breakfast and lunch for most students and play leadership roles in forging school-community connections among services for children and families in need.

Moving forward means changing the mind-set of administrators and teaching staff on how learning takes place. Learning readiness deficits range from a simple inability to sit still and listen to serious developmental delays, some caused by injury to the brain, but most caused by the narrow confines of poverty and social isolation. In response, we tend to make unreasonable demands on teachers. Not only do we expect them to impart information and teach critical thinking but also to function as nurse, counselor, parent, social worker, diagnostician, and police officer. The sad result is chaotic classrooms in which teachers cannot teach and children cannot and will not learn. Implementing coordinated approaches to organizing school resources and developing expertise to meet the diverse needs of students have resulted in significant improvements in teacher and student attitudes about their school and improved student learning.

When the government appears to fail in its mission, we Americans usually turn to the private sector and the competitive business model to solve the problem. This is holding true for education. One solution is alternative programs—schools that are organized by parents, teachers, and community members and funded by public money. These schools offer a unique opportunity to respond to the diverse learning needs of the students. These schools can bring new dimensions to public education and serve as catalysts for systematic change in our traditional systems. A school that holds both the past and the future of the cultural context involved in education is in a better position to work collaboratively with the traditional and emerging sources of wisdom in that culture and to discern and teach the knowledge, skills, and attitudes that the next generation will need as citizens. Schools today must preserve a degree of diversity in order to meet the educational needs of individual students and communities.

To entice our won't learners, schools cannot be mere buildings. They must become contexts that impart socialization messages to children, inviting, empowering, and nurturing them. Schools must become student centered, with support networks to assist students by using community volunteers, parents, teacher aides, and peer tutors to provide individualized learning for students. Academically rich programs, instruction that promotes student learning, collegial interaction, and creative problem solving are components of these schools. This leads to a positive school climate, because there is a partnership between the school and the community. Parents and community members are actively involved in the teaching and learning activities as well as in the decision-making process.

A particularly challenging idea is a call for scaled-up efforts to implement the following:

- Make public schools inclusive and integrated.
- Organize public schools into smaller units.
- Step up research on the needs and learning styles of students.
- Provide a curriculum for all students with a blending of resources and expertise directed to meeting the needs of the individual students.
- Support the needs and concerns of the teachers.
- Forge school connections with family and community.
- Coordinate community resources with exciting resources within the school.

Parents and community members believe that there is a need for new, creative educational models that will be accountable for producing children who are willing to learn, who are functionally literate, and who are prepared to make informal choices in a democratic society. The family becomes an agent for change in the educational process. The community and its connections become agents for change. Relationships between schools and a wide variety of community resources (government agencies, business organizations, religious institutions, and social and medical service agencies) are nurtured and empowered.

As we move forward and take our journey together, educators agree that successful schools that are working with the won't learners have four main goals:

1. Maximize a child's development by integrating various components of learning.
2. Integrate a multidisciplinary approach to curriculum.
3. Serve at-risk students and provide them with a safe, secure environment for learning.
4. Help to break the cycle of poverty by giving students the academic tools they will need to function in the twenty-first century.

The mission of these schools is to provide an opportunity for youth to actively learn in a way that is respectful to individual learning styles, development, and interests; to encourage all students toward high achievement and excellence; and to support family and community participation in each student's education. These schools are dedicated to accelerating the development of inner-city, at-risk students whose potential has been robbed by severe socioeconomic conditions and academic failure. In 1877, Tatanka Iotanko (Chief Sitting Bull, Lakota Sioux) said, "Let us put our minds together and see what life can make for our children." We should listen to these words and take heed.

One of my won't learners, a student of American Indian ancestry, had this to say: "It is time to start learning about things they told you, you did not need to know. Knowing about me instead of learning about them. It's a connection that makes learning education."

We are losing thousands of kids by trying to fit them into systems that prevent learning. Children need to be allowed to find out what they are good at and then be allowed to develop. Change the environment to fit the students. Hire teachers who are sensitive to their students and who will hang in there until the student "gets it."

We can begin our journey together by making life better for children in need. Of all the riches denied to disadvantaged, at-risk, won't learners, perhaps the most important is a network that would allow them to thrive in school and give them a sense of belonging. The lack of this support and the norms and values that underpin it place their education at risk from the first day they walk into a classroom. More than that, their minds and hearts are not filled with the hopes, dreams, and aspirations from which to fashion academic success. They know neither what they are missing nor where to turn to get it, and affliction is apt to continue throughout the duration of their schooling. The won't learners have been denied the experiences that form the foundation on which a formal education is constructed. These learners have not become part of the network that adds to the intellectual enrichment, even of small children.

Those who want to raise educational standards and improve classroom learning must acknowledge, especially so far as the won't learners are concerned, that the out-of-school lives of these learners cannot be ignored. Children spend most of their time beyond the school walls; even inside the school, their learning bears the indelible stamp of outside influences. The underlying support system of students in need has to be shored up so that they will have a sturdy foundation on which to stand. The school should be viewed as part of an ecosystem that includes all parts of a child's life. Families and communities need help if they are to structure relationships that provide children with values and opportunities in harmony with productive learning.

When learners gain a *sense of connectedness* to the people and institutions whose guidance and assistance will help them to advance themselves, their social capital increases. At the same time, they can prosper as learners only if they have emotional and physical underpinnings that provide for their *sense of well-being* and keep them from being overwhelmed by their environments. They need a *sense of academic initiative* to motivate and sustain their scholastic efforts. Finally, a *sense of knowing* allows our students to accrue the academic and social learning that lets them select a path to follow in a society that would otherwise limit them to a choice of no options at all.

A Sense of Connectedness

Schools in inner-city neighborhoods can strengthen ties to students by building links to the community. Harlem's Public School 194 in New York City placed high priority on demonstrating their program's connectedness to the community through such activities as voter registration assistance and block cleanups.

The belief that the school, as an integral part of community improvement, guides almost everything that happens to Ivydale Elementary School in Clay County, West Virginia, where 80 percent of the families qualify for free lunches. Welfare is a way of life for many residents of the area. Ivydale has offered one program after another. Various grants have paid for a preschool, a reading tutor, and a summer camp that is one of the few recreational opportunities in the area. Ivydale also started a program to keep their gym open on Sundays. After-school child care is offered, a GED program exists, and recently construction started on the only tennis court in the county. Elsewhere in America at several charter schools, programs involving school-to-work have opened endless possibilities with for jobs for students, and these programs have developed invaluable contacts within the community.

A Sense of Well-Being

A sense of well-being that America's advantaged children take for granted is missing from the lives of many less-advantaged children. For those who live in the inner city, day-to-day existence is a crapshoot in which they can come up losers with no choice. Little about their lives is predictable save the unsettled nature of their existence. Yet these learners are supposed to involve themselves in serious learning and overcome the adversities that undermine formal schooling.

One way a school can affect children's sense of well-being is to envelop them in its protecting arms. The range of services that some enhancement programs offer students to promote their well-being ranges from medical and dental services to health therapy, drug prevention sessions, tutoring, homework help, mentoring, after-school recreation, and summer programs.

A Sense of Academic Initiative

In neighborhoods in which achievement seems most irrelevant to the rest of their lives, students may receive little support for putting forth effort in the classroom. These learners do not know from an early age what is expected of them academically and where their education is supposed to take them. "These children are expected to fail," said the sponsor of an I Have a Dream Project. "The people they spend most of their time with, their parents and their teachers, have low expectations of them. No one respects them so it is tough for these kids to have any aspirations. The ones who get anywhere are the drug dealers and the athletes."

Self-discipline in the form of good study habits plays a fundamental role in cultivating academic initiative. The acquisition of habits of study groups helps young people to build structure in their lives instead of submitting to unpredictability. Much of the emphasis in the summer REACH program for young black males in Cleveland, Ohio, deals with learning how to learn.

A Sense of Knowing

The won't learners need a sturdy foundation upon which to construct further intellectual attainment. A sense of knowing undergirds academic achievement. Those who know have a firmer basis for knowing more. Affluent parents use their resources to begin the process when infants are still in their cribs and playpens, and it continues throughout childhood. They talk to their infants, read to their toddlers, and ask their growing children questions that prompt conversation. These parents surround their children with experiences that broaden vocabulary and deepen meaning. The development of language benefits from careful nurturing so that knowing how to speak, read, write, and listen with precision can become second nature. Most alternative programs try to erect at least a part of this foundation while, at the same time, attempting to compensate for omissions.

The effects that alternative programs make to achieve parity with more advantaged learners involve building a more elaborate sense of knowing by using extended school days, longer school weeks, and the inclusion of summer in the educational program. This approach calls for giving youngsters safe and productive places to spend the hours outside the regular school day, when they otherwise might be exposed to harm or fall into negative patterns of behavior. Alternative programs also use tutoring, exposure to the arts, coaching for college admissions tests, and visiting community events.

The Children's Aid Society at I.S. 218 in Manhattan pays to keep the library open extra hours. Expo Middle School in St. Paul, Minnesota, offers snacks and recreation to students each day when classes end. Communities in Schools staffs its Giants' Academy in Newark, New Jersey, early in the morning and late in the afternoon so that students can get added practice in basic skills and receive homework help while remaining off the streets. The Beacons Program at P.S. 194 in Harlem includes one-on-one tutoring after school for forty students whose records indicated that they were in danger of failing if they did not receive special attention. Fienberg-Fisher School in Miami Beach, Florida, operates a homework club in response to the wishes of parents who recognize that many of their children live in apartments so small that there is no place to find the solitude that homework demands.

It is no wonder that students who are economically disadvantaged know so little of the larger world. They do not get to the library or the circus. They may participate in little conversation of substance outside school. They are not taken on vacations and they may have met few people other than their teachers who ever attended a play or a classical music concert. A trip to a restaurant means going to McDonald's or Burger King. At some alternative schools, volunteers will take students to restaurants where they can sit down to a meal with a tablecloth and a setting of tableware. This is a first-time experience for many of our students.

COMMON TRAITS OF COMPETENT SCHOOLS

As we ponder where to begin in developing schools to help the won't learners, we look to research (much of it completed by Linda Darling-Hammond) that over the last several decades suggests that schools that develop high levels of both competence and community share nine features: active, in-depth learning organized around common goals; a focus on authentic performance; attention to student development; appreciation for diversity; opportunities for collaborative learning; collaborative perspective across the school; collaborative structures for caring; support for democratic learning; and connections to family and community.

Active, In-depth Learning Organized around Common Goals

Active learning reflects the old saying, "I hear and I forget; I see and I remember; I do and I understand." Active learning aimed at genuine understanding begins with the disciplines, not with whimsical activities detached from core subject-matter concepts. It treats disciplines as alive, not inert. Schools must teach for understanding and engage the students in valuing the works of writers, scientists, mathematicians, musicians, sculptors, and critics in context as realistically as possible, using the criteria of performance in the disciplines as standards toward which students and teachers strive.

Merely creating interesting tasks for students is not enough. Work that results in deep understanding has at least three features:

- It requires the use of higher-order cognitive functions, taking students beyond recall, recognition, and reproduction of information to evaluation, analysis, synthesis, and production of arguments, ideas, and performances.

- It asks our won't learners to apply these skills and ideas in meaningful contexts, engaging them in activities they have real reason to want to undertake.
- It builds upon students' prior learning but presses toward more displaced understandings.

Experiences in taking on problems and developing skilled performances enable students to think and solve problems in other settings.

Four conditions are prevalent for active, in-depth learning. First, curriculum guidance must focus on core concepts and allow for in-depth inquiry rather than demanding the superficial coverage of massive amounts of information. Second, assessments must look for evidence of understanding, not just recall and recognition of information. Third, structures for learning must allow extended blocks of time for teachers and students to work together around meaningful problems in ways that are as authentic as possible. Fourth, teacher evaluation systems must recognize teachers for skillfully managing activity-based learning rather than for only using lecture and recitation models.

Emphasis on Authentic Performance

Authentic performance is critical to the development of competence. Thus, meaningful performances in real-world contexts should become the focus of curriculum and assessment. Both should become so closely intertwined as to be inseparable. Authentic performance is showing competency in real-life situations (e.g., in math class, doing a budget, or in social studies, being aware and knowledgeable in current events).

Attention to Development

Schools should be user friendly. Class assignments should build upon children's normal developmental dispositions so that student and teacher energy can be turned to the pursuit of relevant learning rather than wasted on an adversarial process of unnatural behavior management. In user-friendly schools and classrooms, teachers select intrinsically motivating activities that enable students to master their environment, are appropriate to students' stages of growth, and address common curriculum goals. Activities alternate between relatively short periods of whole-group instruction and longer stretches of work time when students engage in different tasks suited to their individual readiness and needs.

The benefits of developmental attentiveness do not stop after the early years. In a 1998 review of research on the education of early adolescents, Braddock and McPartland argue that many well-known adolescent difficulties are not intrinsic to the teenage years but are related to the mismatch between adolescents' developmental needs and the kinds of experiences most middle and high schools provide. When students need close affiliation, they experience large depersonalized schools; when they need to develop autonomy, they experience few opportunities for choice and punitive approaches to discipline; when they need expansive cognitive challenges and opportunities to demonstrate their competence, they are given assignments focused largely on the memorization of facts; when they need to build self-confidence and a healthy identity, they experience teaching that labels many of them as academically deficient. Many students who entered middle school feeling good about school leave persuaded that they do not count and cannot learn.

Appreciation for Diversity

Howard Gardner's contemporary intelligence theory confirms what is obvious when we look at human accomplishments: that people possess a complex mix of intelligences that are developed over time in cultural contexts and are used in various ways.

Successful schools give students an opportunity to develop each of the seven intelligences Gardner describes: logical-mathematical, musical, spatial, interpersonal, intrapersonal, bodily, and linguistic. Teachers look for ways to identify and build on learner strengths by addressing learners' use of visual, verbal, auditory, and tactile senses and by using deductive and inductive approaches to learning. This provides pathways to success for won't learners who, in traditional classrooms, would be marked for failure, yet it does not avoid the need to develop skills across all areas. When students start from the strategies they find comfortable, they can achieve success in learning that ultimately enables them to expand their repertoire of skills and approaches.

Opportunities for Collaborative Learning

Collaboration between and among students and teachers is at the core of schools where diversity enhances learning, just as it is in the new work environment where teams pool knowledge. Collaboration allows both children and adults to verbalize and sharpen thinking as they teach one another.

Bruce Turnbaugh, a thirty-five-year veteran of the teaching force, defines collaboration as a combination of individual and small-group work in an environment in which variety allows us to capitalize on differences. Students have a role model in the classroom and assistance from peers. Students in Turnbaugh's classes learn to meet high expectations in an atmosphere where they are allowed to expand their responsibility to each other. Bruce says that groups are important because students need to use language to learn language. They need to talk with each other. They need to read instructions, and to have the opportunity to repeat, review, and listen. "The focus is on students' learning rather than on me teaching. . . . The goal is for students to assume responsibility for their own learning and to discover how they learn best," says Turnbaugh.

A Collaborative Perspective across the School

Research on extraordinarily successful schools has found that these schools have forged a sense of mission, a shared ethos, and common norms of instruction and civility, in contrast to those schools with individualistic norms.

When common goals and commitments motivate school life, learning becomes more powerful because it is cumulative rather than disjointed. Students and teachers work toward habits that are practical, reinforced, and supported until they become second nature. Rather than switching mind-sets several times each day and many times over the course of a school career, students can concentrate on developing their abilities and teachers can collaborate with each other in helping them do so.

Structures for Caring

The process of engaging school members in discourse and decision making builds thoughtfulness and respect that translate into positive social learning. Developing more humane and psychologically healthy schools requires school structures and strategies that allow for the enactment of caring and the teaching of caring. These depend, in turn, on policies that strengthen education preparation, promote personalization of schools so that greater intimacy and understanding are possible, and establish a curriculum that develops respect and empathy.

At one alternative school, the seven values of the Ojibwe (love, respect, courage, honesty, wisdom, humility, and truth) are the basis of the curriculum. Jennifer Coughlin, school counselor, says, "If we want kids to be caring and compassionate, then we must provide a place for growing up in which effective care is feasible. Caring and compassion are part of the hard core of subjects we are responsible for teaching" (March 28, 2001).

Support for Democratic Learning

We need democratic schools that seek to create as many shared experiences and as many avenues of discourse for diverse groups of students as possible. Such schools not only provide a more individualized education with greater learning opportunities and markedly better outcomes but also respond to the need all learners feel to find a place in which their experiences can be acknowledged and affirmed. A democratic pedagogy supports freedom of expression, inclusion of multiple perspectives, a chance to evaluate ideas and make choices, and opportunities to take on responsibility and contribute to the greater good. Because democracy must be lived to be learned, democratic classrooms can be developed only in inclusive organizations that encourage broad participation of students, parents, teachers, and community members.

Many schools have already developed policies that encourage the accommodation of diversity in the classroom. Teachers develop discipline policies and construct pedagogues that allow for student participation. Learner- and learning-centered classrooms and curriculum enhance the activities at these schools.

Connections to Family and Community

Although it is important for parents to be represented on decision-making committees and involved in setting school direction, what parents most need and want are closer connections to the learning process for their children. Many schools allow teachers to build parental support for and understanding of classroom assignments through parent conferences, reviews, and displays of students' work, along with involvement in classroom activities. When parents are engaged and when students and their work are at the center of the conversation, teachers and parents can focus together on how their children are learning. Both can offer observations about learners' strategies, paces and styles of learning, their different strengths and experiences, the ways they express what they know or don't know, and the kinds of teaching strategies effective for them. When teachers' insights are supported by parents' insights, teachers can more easily connect learners' experiences to curriculum goals.

The following interviews are from men and women who are gaining national recognition in the field of alternative education. Each one is planting and growing the seeds of educational reform for the twenty-first century. All the interviewees (during conversations from June through October 2001) said that curriculum and learning environment is critical in making schools unique for the won't learners.

Joe Nathan, director of the Center for School Change, says, "Schools are out of sync with the real world. They do not take into consideration how students learn. Therefore, kids do not want to attend school."

Nancy Smith, former director of the New Twin City Charter School Movement, says, "Lack of culturally appropriate teaching methods and curriculum materials leads to underachievement, absenteeism, high dropout rates, and the lack of parental involvement. We are learning that we have to do things in a different way. The traditional system does not work for the won't learners."

Russell Means, Indian activist, says, "Many Indian kids are won't learners. We are social, interactive learners. We watch how others do it and see if it will work for us. We check out ideas, argue, bounce ideas back and forth. We talk. Talk lies at the heart of everyday life and intellectual development. This exchange is rarely allowed in traditional

American schools. We must create the most effective learning environments that we can."

The experts also mentioned that parent involvement is necessary for successful learning. Dr. Lloyd Elm, director of the American Indian Magnet School in St. Paul, Minnesota, says, "Show the parents something positive and they will believe in you. Lack of parental concern for their child's learning can harm the student."

Finally, the experts mentioned class and school size as being important factors in student learning. Russell Means says, "Downsize the school and restructure the classroom to allow for small group learning activities and our won't learners will thrive."

Joe Nathan says, "I believe kids are leaving the traditional schools because of size. Schools are too large and the kids are unable to handle the bigness."

Milo Cutter, director of the City Academy Charter School in St. Paul, Minnesota (the nation's first charter school), says, "The small size of a school is a strength. More and more youngsters do not fit in large schools. We know it. We have to do something about it."

Steve Chapman, director of Indian Education, Minneapolis Public Schools, says, "Small size is a strength. Won't learners within the Indian community thrive in a small classroom. I see it as the one-room schoolhouse effect. The children are treated like part of a family. This goes back to our heritage. There is a huge sense of comfort in 'small.' All students can benefit from smaller classes and schools."

System change becomes possible when individuals with different roles interact around shared concern for student learning.

HOW DO WE BEGIN?

We begin by looking at the schools around us. Small schools are cited as an important factor when parents choose a school for their children. The increasing size of traditional American schools, especially the large comprehensive high schools with more than 1,000 students, creates conditions conductive to dropping out. Won't learners who had attended large schools were placed in large classes and often followed a low academic or nonacademic tract. When these students enrolled in a small school

with smaller classes, their academics and attendance improved. Small-
ness also permits the human connections that result in strong student-
teacher bonds, enabling the school to affect personal issues like drug
abuse, life plan aspiration, and post high school behavior.

It was, sadly, the Columbine High killings in suburban Denver in
1999 that may have provided the most dramatic evidence in the case
against big schools. In the aftermath, many blamed the violence on
Columbine's immense size (2,000 students) and the powerful cliques
that evolve in such an environment. Critics included Al Gore, who
blasted the practice of "herding all students into overcrowded, factory-
style high schools."

And yet the case for small schools doesn't just rest on emotional rhet-
oric and bloody television footage. Recent studies have shown that simply reducing the size of a school can "create small, supportive learning
environments that give students a sense of connection," as Richard Ri-
ley, former U.S. Secretary of Education, put it. "And it's not just a feel-
good environment for students." Stacy Mitchell of the Institute for Local Self-Reliance reports that students in urban, rural, and suburban
schools (300–400 students for elementary schools, 400–600 for middle
schools, and 400–800 for high schools) outdo their big school peers in
grades and test scores, have far fewer discipline problems and lower
dropout rates, and log more years in postsecondary education.

Buoyed by these and other findings, the U.S. Department of Education, in October 2000, awarded grants to 354 schools in 39 states to help
create smaller, more personalized "learning communities," including
"schools within schools" in large high schools. Meanwhile, state education officials around the country are finally beginning to see the value of
the small schools that have survived the consolidation trend of the 1980s
and 1990s.

All of this elates Deborah Meier, whose pioneer small schools in
Harlem helped inspire a boom in New York City, which now boasts
more than 100 small schools. "It's not even their particular approach
to curriculum and pedagogy that makes them work," writes Meier in
The Nation (June 5, 2000). "It's that the schools are organized to maximize the power of the adults who know the kids best, the strength of
their ties with the kids and families, and their ability to put together
a coherent schoolwide pedagogy and curriculum. And," she adds, "all

of this can happen inside the public sector, without charters, vouchers, or privatization."

Still, Meier doubts that the "bigger is better" ethos that sprang up during the 1950s will soon disappear. As Philip Langdon notes in the conservative journal, *The American Enterprise* (January 2000), many educators, parents, and students still believe big schools are better able to offer modern equipment and advanced curriculums.

However, small-school proponents can poke holes in just about every "bigger is better" argument. Small schools may not offer as many classes, they argue, but their teachers generally have more flexibility to incorporate sophisticated material as well as the freedom to use innovative teaching methods, such as multiage classrooms. While big schools can offer deluxe sports facilities and busy extracurricular rosters, smaller schools have a higher participation rate, meaning that more students will get the leadership training and improved academic standing often associated with such activities. Parent participation, too, is higher in small schools. Smaller schools may be an answer for our won't learners.

Learning Styles

How do we begin? We begin by looking at threads of learning styles.

Theoretical discussions of learning styles as a focus of presentation and study have become part of the vernacular in educational reform. A sense of optimism suggests that an understanding of learning styles is one of the keys to understanding the school experience for our won't learners. Policymakers, administrators, teachers, parents, and students have become sophisticated thinkers and users of the knowledge being generated about learning styles and teaching styles. The term "learning styles," however, has different meanings for people. For some, it is synonymous with "cognitive styles"; for others, it refers to preferred approaches to learning based on modality strengths; still others believe it means hemispheric functioning, such as right-brain or left-brain.

Won't learners exhibit some important differences in learning styles. The manner in which a student learns and the way that learning is demonstrated are influenced by the values, activities, and child-rearing practices of the students' home culture. How students process information from the environment is affected by learning styles. Many students are visual learners. Thus, demonstration and modeling by teachers and peers is a helpful strategy to use. Others are global learners and make their decisions based on emotions and intuitions. Some are kinesthetic (recalling what they experience), tactile (recalling what they touch), or auditory and need to hear how and what to do. Won't learners are also socially oriented and will perform better in settings that encourage dialogue and the development of a more personal relationship with the teacher. A won't learner can learn best if he or she is immersed in diverse experiences and is given the opportunity to actively process what he or she has learned.

Observation, imitation, and direct experience of real-world activities make learning a meaningful experience. Abstract, verbal instruction is alien to the won't learners. Presenting classroom materials in an analytic, sequential manner is not useful. The emphasis in many beginning reading programs on a sequential, phonetic approach is why many of our won't learners have difficulty reading.

Differences in learning styles among children in our classrooms should not be seen as insurmountable obstacles. The content of lessons can remain the same, but the strategies used to reach goals and objectives may need to be altered.

Parents and students interviewed about learning styles had this to say:

- "My daughter is a hands-on, real-world, discovery learner."
- "My son needs to be able to use his hands to draw, build, or manipulate."
- "Children need to be allowed to find out what they are good at and then be allowed to develop in that area. My son needs to be actively involved in his lessons."
- "I recall what I see and learn by watching others."
- "I need physical activity as I learn. I need to use my body, to feel. My feeling helps me learn."
- "I need to see the whole picture or hear the whole story first. I start with the end result and then go to the specific. I go back and pick up the missing pieces.
- "I see, I hear, I do."
- "My daughter learns best when engaged in projects, homework, or using a small-group discussion format. She is a risk taker."

Two of the parents summarized their feelings:

"All children can learn. I believe this. In our past, children in the tribe had their own special area. Some were warriors, others spoke for the people, some hunted, and others stayed back and did domestic chores. Each has his or her place. You must help our children find their place."

"Learning styles can be both reflective and active, verbal and nonverbal, concrete and abstract, head and heart. Why can't the traditional school system see that?"

Alternative Education Programs

Many educators are beginning to see alternative educational programs as a huge leap forward with options for providing children with a variety of valuable alternatives and for providing teachers with equally valuable alternatives for creative and successful teaching.

New schools are emerging where the following key elements combine synergistically to produce an array of educational opportunities aimed at meeting the demands and needs of the won't learner:

- Educational visionaries and leaders are empowered to create learning environments driven by a set of beliefs and sensitivity to what prospective parents and students are seeking.
- Teachers are empowered to create settings aligned with their personal and professional beliefs of how best to teach and where their expertise, knowledge, and input really count as important toward the achievement and progress of the students they interact with.
- Parents are empowered and their voices hold schools accountable for doing what they say they will do.
- Students are able to benefit from such educational environment because these schools have been created with the student in mind and where students' needs supercede all others.

With these elements in mind, we need to change the way we think about, as well as provide for, the education, learning, and freedom of choice for the won't learners.

How much do we really know about initiating, implementing, and sustaining educational change? If we ask groups of teachers, principals, district leaders, state education officials, legislators, parents, corporations, and local business communities, each may respond differently. Since the late 1970s, we have amassed an extensive body of knowledge about educational reform. Whether or not we choose to heed this knowledge, the answers are "blowing in the wind," as composer and musician Bob Dylan wrote in 1962 when he questioned our inability to act in the Vietnam War era. Dylan asked, "How many times must a man look up before he sees the sky? . . . The answer is blowing in the wind." Are our answers blowing in the wind when it comes to helping our won't learners?

Several decades after Dylan's disturbing question, we are engaged in an equally important social problem: the struggle to find ways to implement and sustain educational changes and make a significant difference in the lives of children. The questions that educators might ask are similar to Dylan's in their ethical implications. For example, *how many times* can we continue to enact policies that fly in the face of years of research about change? *How many times*, when the future of millions of children is at stake, can we continue not to act on all that we know about educational change?

Educational reform at the school level requires leadership and a reform-support infrastructure. The seeds of change must be nourished in a climate of respectful and open dialogue. If we are to effectively help our won't learners, we must be willing to dialogue, which, in turn, leads directly to a reform-support infrastructure.

Many alternative schools work to ensure equitable opportunities and outcomes for all students regardless of their socioeconomic status, race, ethnicity, or gender. These schools believe in student voices where the students themselves have a critical role to play in helping the schools become rigorous and caring places. These schools believe in professional development as a critical link between educational reform and improved student outcomes. These schools also believe in community engagement, which can be defined to include parents as well as such partners as colleges, universities, and community-based organizations, as a critical component of school reform. Finally, these schools use a curriculum that emphasizes the goal of ensuring equitable opportunities and outcomes as a critical lens for assessing the effectiveness of particular programs and instructional approaches.

Our won't learners will respond to:

- School programs where they can be actively engaged in pursuing learning
- Teachers who are highly committed to the students and their learning
- A school that is distinctive, reflecting an identity or "personality" of its own
- A program where there is a collegial interaction and collaboration among teachers, reflecting a staff that forms a professional community
- Teachers who have extended roles, serving students not only as instructors but also as advisors, mentors, confidants, and friends
- More course content offered for everyone, in contrast to a curriculum divided into tracks
- A program with holistic arms, demonstrating concern with students' personal and social development as well as with academics
- A school that reflects self-consciousness of itself as a community, establishing expectations of its members and making commitments to them
- A school with an explicit purpose, identifying a mission, particular set of goals, content, and instructional orientation
- A school that is empowered to set its own direction with teachers making critical decisions

As we begin working with our won't learners, we need to focus on five major "intellectual habits." These habits should be internalized by every student, and used no matter what they are studying about, both in school and especially out of school! These five "habits," advocated for and used by Deborah Meier, director of Central Park East Schools in East Harlem, New York City, include concern for evidence (How do you know that?), viewpoint (Who said it and why?), cause and effect (What led to it? What else happened?), and hypothesizing (What if? Supposing that?).

But most important is the fifth habit: Who cares? Knowing and learning take on importance only when we are convinced it matters, that it really makes a difference. Having a good mind and being well educated do not always seem important at fifteen years of age.

Our won't learners are in a great deal of conflict between their ambitions, their compassion for others, and their loyalties to family and friends. It is important for won't learners to be able to stand alone and to take personal responsibility; it is also important to learn to work together and to collaborate with others.

Many of our won't learners are "square-peg" kids who do not readily fit into the round holes of conventional schools. The focus is on students, boys and girls in trouble with the law, dropouts, and others who have difficulty thriving in traditional schools. These are learners who can legitimately be described as having needs that the traditional public schools have been unsuccessful in meeting.

Many at-risk and disadvantaged students need alternative ways to learn. Schools must be in a position to provide the social and emotional skills that students need to help avoid disaffection, dropping out because of poor academic performance (inability to read, write, or perform mathematical computations), attendance issues, self-destructive behaviors including drug and alcohol abuse, or gang involvement. Individualized curriculum, experiential learning, and smaller class sizes are the focus of many innovative schools and are useful tools for our won't learners.

It appears that everyone wants to improve schooling in America, but each in a different way. Some want to strengthen basic skills, others critical thinking. Some want to promote citizenship or character, others want to warn against the dangers of drugs and violence. Some programs demand more from parents, others accept the role of the community. Some emphasize core values, others the need to respect diversity. All, however, realize that schools play an essential role in preparing students to become knowledgeable, responsible, and caring adults.

Won't learners must become *knowledgeable*. They should be ready and motivated to learn and capable of integrating new information into their lives. They must become *responsible*. Won't learners should be able to understand risks and opportunities and be motivated to choose actions and behaviors that serve their own interests and those of others. Won't learners also must become *caring*. They should be able to see beyond themselves, appreciate the concerns of others, and come to believe that to care is to be part of a community that is welcoming, nurturing, and concerned about their lives. Caring is central to the shaping of relationships that are important, meaningful, supportive, rewarding, and productive. At-risk students are most vulnerable for growing up without caring. The value that most Americans find necessary in adult life is caring. Adults agree that caring is rooted in the emotional and social development of a child.

Experience and research show that promoting social and emotional development in children is "the missing piece" in efforts to reach the array of goals associated with improving school programs in the United States. Social and emotional competence is the ability to understand, manage, and express the social and emotional aspects of one's life in ways that enable the successful management of life skills, such as learning, forming relationships, solving everyday problems, and adapting to the complex demands of growth and development. Our won't learners should learn self-awareness strategies, impulsivity control, working cooperatively, and caring about oneself and others.

As we prepare youth for the challenges of life in our complex and fast-paced world, it appears that the real challenge of education is no longer *whether* or *not* to attend to the social and emotional life of the learner, but how to attend to the social and emotional issues in education.

We must realize that every young person has a deep need to belong. Our won't learners, often with the greatest need for relationships, are the most alienated from adults and peers. Our job is to help them make a planned and concerted effort to nourish inviting relationships in a culture of belonging. Only then can learning take place.

6

TIPS FOR SUCCESS

We never know, believe me, when we have succeeded best.

—Miguel de Unamuno

Today's attack on adolescents is angry and punishing. Teenagers are blamed for nearly all major social ills: poverty, welfare, dependence, crime, gun violence, suicide, sexual promiscuity, unwed motherhood, AIDS, school failure, broken families, child abuse, drug abuse, drunken driving, smoking, and the breakdown of "family values." Adolescent personality evokes in adults, conflict, anxiety, and intense hostility (usually disguised as concern).

The United States has the highest rate of children and adolescents living in families with incomes below the poverty guidelines ($11,522 per year for a family of three in 1999) in the industrial world, the result of spending fewer public resources on children than any other industrial nation.

Youth is by far our poorest age-group. One in four is impoverished, twice the rate among adults according to the 1999 Census Bureau. According to the National Center on Child Abuse and Neglect, this totals 16 million children and teens who live in poverty. Where race, ethnicity, and gender were central to past social conflicts, young age has become a major new factor.

Adolescence is a time of turbulence marked by rapid physical, sexual, social, and emotional development. It is a time of confusion and rebellion. Adults, in turn, have regarded adolescents with hope and foreboding throughout this past century. The message the 1990s American adults have sent to our youth is, "You are not our kids. We do not care about you." America's legacy to its young people includes bad schools, poor health care, deadly addictions, crushing debts, and utter indifference.

Wake up, America. You know that you live in uncommon times for educators when everyone from President George W. Bush to the Children's Defense Fund is championing the same slogan, "Leave No Child Behind." To increase the achievement levels of our won't learners, we need to focus on what really matters: high standards, a challenging real-life curriculum, and good teachers.

As clouded as the prospects for urban education may appear, the nation has not given up on these learners. On the contrary, scores of efforts are under way across the United States to help urban school districts and our won't learners hit the ever-moving target of twenty-first-century achievement.

Because of the problem of student achievement, the boldest experiments in American education are playing out in urban areas. In hopes of narrowing the achievement gap between the won't learners and our "normal" students, reformers are looking to everything from providing tuition vouchers to closing failing schools.

"The impetus for these radical changes is not coming from complacent learners," says Chester E. Finn Jr., president of the Thomas Fordham Foundation in Washington D.C., and a senior fellow at the Indianapolis-based Hudson Institute (Wasley, et al. 2000). It is coming from the most discontented and disaffected part of the population, the won't learners who are trapped in lousy, unchanging school systems.

The question remains, what can we do to fix these schools and help the won't learners?

Research suggests that efforts to reduce class size (especially in the early grades) and to provide early childhood education reap the largest benefits for poor and minority students, many of whom represent our won't learners. Data also suggest that students who score at the bottom of the heap are the most amenable to change.

Equally important will be the willingness and ability of state governments to strike the right balance between pressure and support. State officials can no longer afford to dismiss urban educational problems as "local control" issues beyond the scope of state policy.

SUCCESSFUL STRATEGIES

Despite the clouded prospects for urban learners, there are schools of excellence being created against often debilitating odds. These triumphs have given rise to justifiable faith that with enough perseverance and political will, the problems of urban education and the won't learners may prove solvable after all. No one says it is going to be easy. What follows is an overview of some strategies being pursued around the country to make that hope a reality. These strategies become a series of tips for success, some general and philosophical, others more specific. All strategies will work in interested schools throughout the country when modified and adapted to fit local communities.

Raise the Bar

Set clear, high expectations for all students. "Why do we have to do this?" The question may irritate the teacher, but it is one of the most intelligent questions that a student can ask. Students (and the rest of us, for that matter) are loath to expend cognitive energy unnecessarily. Assessing the importance of a task is a key initial step in learning. Therefore, understanding the importance of emotions and feelings is crucial to effective teaching and learning. Children learn best if they are immersed in complex experiences and are given the opportunity to actively process what they have learned. There is no reason why students could not learn writing skills as part of a journalism class, or properties of chemicals and their interaction as a part of an environmental project, or better understand some mathematical concepts by seeing them applied to a business or energizing problem. We need to look at the fact that research has uncovered the disturbing result that American high school students are performing at a lower rate and level on standardized tests than their peers in many countries. We need a plan of action.

Make Performance Count

Schools need to devise an accountable system based on accurate information. Never before has the public demand for results in education been so high. Principals cannot ignore any group in their school. They must pay close attention to student performance. That is the key to accountability.

Let Leaders Lead

Create clear lines of authority. Give schools the freedom that they need in exchange for accountability and allow those at the top of the pyramid the flexibility to do their jobs.

Recruit for Success

Recruit, hire, and retain teachers who will enable the students to reach high standards. The situation is often unfair. Children with the most urgent needs often wind up with teachers who are the least prepared to meet these needs.

Support Your Local Teachers

Build in capacities at the ground level to improve teaching and learning, with a strong focus on improved curriculum and instruction. A school is only as strong as the teaching staff that works there. What really counts is interaction between the teacher and the student.

Go the Extra Mile

Give students the extra time and attention they need to be successful. As the drive for higher standards marches on, we are under mounting pressure to do whatever it takes to help our students make the grade. After-school tutoring programs, a focus on early literacy (make all students literate by the third grade), summer school, year-round school, preschool initiatives, and smaller classes are some of the ways we can respond to the challenge.

Reach Out

Improve the relationship between parents and community with schools and educators. We need to redefine schools as community anchors. There is ample evidence in support of the value of school-community partnerships. Programs report that making a range of services available in schools can help reduce student discipline referrals, absenteeism, and course failures. Studies also show that outside actors, particularly the business community, have been a powerful force in efforts to decentralize and reform school bureaucracies.

Employ Aggressive Efforts

Seek out additional means of support, financial and in-kind. A partnership with an insurance company brought one school donated computers. A partnership with a local bank resulted in a school receiving a fifteen-passenger van. A partnership with a law firm, a company looking to adopt a school, brought sponsorship for a local drug awareness week. An architectural firm provides treats on holidays. A local sorority mounts fund-raisers and helps foot the bill for special needs, such as new library books. Some partnerships provide tutoring programs in which employees work with "study buddies" on math and reading.

Set Priorities

Place an emphasis on what is essential to know and on drawing connections between subjects. Do not just "cover the material." For example, because not all students progress at the same rate, teachers should be allowed to give "differentiated credits." In the same math classroom, this means that some of the students earn an algebra credit, while others emerge with pre-algebra on their record. Students who do not earn full credit as ninth graders are encouraged to take another class to master credit in the tenth grade.

Emphasize Class Meetings

Class meetings teach essential skills and empower young people to develop a positive attitude for success in all areas of life (school, work, family, and community). Effective class meetings prepare students for responsible citizenship. Students learn social skills (listening, taking turns, hearing different points of view, negotiating, communicating, helping each other, and taking responsibility for their own behaviors). They also strengthen their academic skills, perhaps without realizing it. During class meetings, students learn oral language skills, attentiveness, critical-thinking skills, decision-making skills, problem-solving skills, and democratic procedures, all of which will enhance their academic performance.

Think Small

Shrink the size of classes and schools. For years, the research has gone back and forth on the impact of class size on student achievement. Now this research seems to be sitting on the side of smaller classes, especially in the inner-city schools.

Think small, but acknowledge that size isn't everything. Smaller, nontraditional schools offer a sanctuary from the larger, more violence-prone, inner-city schools. However, even ardent proponents of scaled-down schooling agree that simply being small is not enough. Many call it a prerequisite for creating a climate in which teachers and students know each other well, bureaucracy is kept at bay, and innovative and personalized forms of teaching and learning flourish.

Research in small school settings has consistently found that there is better attendance, lower dropout rates, fewer incidents of violence, and greater after-school participation, according to Kathleen Cotton, an Oregon researcher who analyzed the findings of 103 earlier studies and reviews. Her 1996 analysis also found that students in smaller schools have more positive attitudes toward academics and that poor and minority students gained the most from small settings.

In a small setting, we can give the students a demanding yet achievable dream, and provide them with road maps and partners for reaching their goals. One high school student, Heather, said that she believed her social life was ruined when she was asked to leave her traditional high school.

> If I went to school with the same kids, especially a bunch of puny guys all my own age, how was I ever going to get a date? But I went. I had the same teachers for core subjects and I got to know the other kids really well. The teachers cared for me and started telling me that I was a good writer. The kids did too. They really pushed me hard. Soon I was helping other kids. Before long, I began to believe in myself, that I could be a good writer. Now I am going to college. Stephen King, look out. (Heather is a recent high school graduate.)

Heather's positive experience in a small alternative high school is similar to the experiences of many other graduates of intentionally small high schools. Her school of 250 students was created by educators who wanted to get to know their students, challenge them, and make sure that no student fell through the cracks. Since the mid-1980s, educators have been creating small schools in New York City, Chicago, Boston, Philadelphia, Los Angeles, Houston, and other urban areas. Together, parents, teachers, and principals have found these small schools better able to engage the intellectual and emotional lives of students and to improve students' academic performance. As the number of small schools has grown throughout the 1990s, the body of research has also grown, in both breadth and depth, enough to make the case for small schools compelling, if not irrefutable.

For decades, similar data have been available but largely ignored by policymakers. During the late 1990s, however, shootings at large high schools made people realize that the structures, daily routines, and impersonal relationships of large schools had created cultures where significant numbers of students were disengaged in the life of the school and alienated from adults and one another.

In Chicago, small schools have been proliferating since 1994. Each of these approximately 150 small schools serves 200 to 400 students. Located in the poorest neighborhoods in the city, they take shape as schools within larger schools, as free-standing schools in their own buildings with their own principals, or as redesigned large schools with one principal but containing several smaller, independent schools, each with its own lead teacher. These small schools were created to remove the sense of isolation and to reduce the gap between the performance of poorer and, too often, minority students and the more affluent students in the district.

A study by Roger Wasley and several colleagues in 2000 found that students in ninety small Chicago high schools made significant improvements in school behavior and achievement. For example, compared with students in host schools, students in these alternative environments attended up to five more days of school per semester; dropped out at one-third to one-half the rate (in newer small schools, 4.8 percent compared to 12.9 percent); had up to 0.22 higher grade point averages; and improved reading scores by the equivalent of almost half a year.

Students reported feeling safer and more connected with adults in small schools. Teachers reported a greater sense of efficacy, job satisfaction, and connection with parents, as well as more opportunities to collaborate with other teachers, build a coherent educational program, use a variety of instructional approaches, and engage students in peer critique and analysis. Parents and community members reported increased confidence in the schools.

Other studies of small schools report similar findings. In one study, for example, "disadvantaged students in small schools significantly outperformed those in large schools on standardized basic skills tests" (Raywid 1997/1998). Small schools were better able to close the achievement gap, especially between less affluent students and their more affluent counterparts. Small schools were safer, reporting fewer fights and no incidents of serious violence. Students from small schools tended to complete more years of high school and accumulate more credits. With such consistent findings, we need to look more closely at how small schools foster student achievement.

What makes small schools work? Size alone does not make a school good, but it does appear to be an important factor in creating more effective schools. Small size, fewer than 400 students, makes possible certain structures and practices that are conductive to student learning:

- Relationships between students and adults are strong and ongoing.
- Relationships between parents and schools are strong and ongoing.

- The school's organization is flat, with broadly distributed leadership. (Principals or directors often teach part of the day and teachers make administrative decisions about matters directly affecting students.)
- Most small schools do not attempt to be comprehensive. Instead, small schools concentrate on a few goals and insist that all students meet them, finding ways to honor student choice through the development of projects or other learning activities, within a course rather than through an extensive course catalogue.
- Professional development is ongoing, embedded, and site specific.
- The school develops its own culture. (The culture revolves around hard work, high expectations, respect for others, and the expectation that all students will succeed.)
- Smaller schools engage the community in educating young people.

Students, educators, and parents have long recognized the need to bridge the gap between learning experiences in the classroom and the applied skills of the workplace. Students are given the opportunity to work as an intern alongside an adult mentor in order to learn skills and behaviors that are appropriate in the workplace. Students are encouraged to look at their values, skills, and interests and to discover the kinds of jobs most compatible with them. Students become self-reliant and self-confident when allowed to follow their own individual plans.

In schools where attendance is a serious matter, students use a buddy system where one student checks with another each morning to ensure that both get to school. When students skip, they are called and teachers drive to the homes of absent students to bring them to school. When students have perfect attendance for a month, a free pizza lunch is offered.

Start Early

School districts typically eschew early intervention programs as too expensive and wait until kids are failing, in trouble, and dropping out before they are willing to spend money for improvement but it is often too late. Research shows students' home backgrounds are responsible for roughly half of their school achievement. Early intervention gives learners a better start.

Focus on Reading and Mathematics

Many educators applaud former President Clinton's goal of making sure every child can read by the third grade. However, researchers say the critical time comes even earlier. Kids who are not reading by the end of first grade face eight-to-one odds against ever catching up. This may be the reason why our won't learners fight reading.

Bring in Tutors

Students who have yet to attain the academic and social competencies required to succeed in school are caught in an academic gap. They face the possibility of being undereducated, underemployed, and underprepared to participate successfully in the twenty-first century. Society's failure to address the needs of these students dooms many to a life of depending on other people for a living.

In response to this serious challenge, parents and educators are searching for ways to increase the academic competence of students. Tutoring programs in which teachers, para-educators, and other adults provide one-to-one support to reduce the gap between what students are expected to know and what they actually know and can do are important. Several studies have indicated that early one-to-one intervention with a teacher can set kids on the right academic track.

Strategic tutoring is one example of a successful program for our won't learners. This program uses a study-skills approach that teaches students how to become independent learners.

A four-step approach is used. Student knowledge is assessed, followed by constructing or learning a new strategy. The tutor then teaches the strategy by modeling how to use it, checking student understanding, and providing support. The final phase is called transferring, during which the tutor helps plan for the independent application of the strategies.

As educators search for effective methods to improve the performance and quality of life for at-risk, won't learners, strategic tutoring can help close the gap between failure and success for these learners.

Invest in Teachers

"Every dollar you spend on improving the quality of teachers has a bigger effect on student achievement than any other dollar you spend," says Linda Darling-Hammond (1997), executive director of the National Commission on Teaching and America's Future. After reviewing hundreds of research reports, she says the commission "determined that the single-most important determinant of how students achieve is their teachers' qualifications."

Research also shows that new teachers and their students do better when they have the support of experienced teachers in a mentoring program. Without good support, many promising teachers wind up dropping out of teaching or running away from the schools.

Increase the Amount of Time Spent Learning

The more you study, the more you learn. There are lots of ways to extend learning time: longer school days, year-round schools, and evening programs.

Set Goals and Assess Student Progress

Almost every state has set academic standards for their students and many districts have added their own goals to the mix, but all this means nothing if you do not check to see how students are doing in pursuit of these goals.

"But even assessments do not mean much without accountability," says Allan Odden, a University of Wisconsin–Madison professor and codirector for Policy Research in Education. "Accountability," he says, "means (a) you identify your most valued results, (b) you measure them, and (c) you provide incentives or sanctions" (Darling-Hammond 1997). Emphasis on competencies in both instruction and assessment instills high standards and expectations in both teachers and students. In other words, encourage active learning and developmental thinking.

Support Teachers' Professional Development

Research indicates a strong professional development program is at the heart of every lasting school improvement program. Weak professional development programs (drive-by workshops) simply waste the teachers' time and cost school districts thousands of dollars.

Too often, teachers are herded into a half-day workshop in something that they do not care about, that they did not ask for, and that does not relate to problems that they perceive important.

Schools that adopt curriculum programs with a strong record of improving student achievement invest heavily in professional development. Research also stresses that the most effective professional development programs are the ones teachers seek out or develop themselves. A teacher who has an adopted child with Fetal Alcohol Syndrome gave one of the best workshops an alternative school offered. She gave firsthand knowledge of the syndrome and strategies that worked for her. A strong program provides a rich learning environment where teachers can design plans, bring in inside or outside consultants, and work with colleagues over a long period of time about specific subjects for specific age-groups.

The National Staff Development Council (NSDC) has initiated standards for teacher-staff development that focus on the three key categories of context, process, and content. The council argues that all categories must be in place to ensure that staff development makes a difference in student learning. Successful schools believe that even strong research-based content with no attention to follow-up (process) or leadership support (context) will not result in improved student learning.

The context standards within professional development:

- Requires and fosters the norm of continuous improvement
- Requires strong leadership in order to obtain continuing support and to motivate all staff, parents, and the community to be advocates for continuous improvement
- Provides adequate time during the workday for staff to learn and work together to accomplish the individual schools' mission and goals
- Is an innovation in itself that requires study of the change process

Process standards within professional development:

- Provide knowledge skills and attitudes regarding organizational development and systems thinking
- Are based on knowledge about human learning and development
- Provide for three phases of the change process (initiation, implementation, and institutionalization)
- Base priorities on a careful analysis of student data regarding goals for student learning
- Use content that has proven value in increasing student learning and development
- Provide a framework for integrating innovations and relating those innovations to the mission of the organization
- Require an evaluation process that is ongoing, includes multiple sources of information, and focuses on all levels of the school
- Use a variety of staff development approaches to accomplish the goals of improving instruction and student success
- Provide the follow-up necessary to ensure improvement
- Require staff members to learn and apply collaborative skills to make shared decisions, solve problems, and work collegially

The content standards within professional development:

- Increase administrators' and teachers' understanding of how to provide school environment and instruction that are responsive to the developmental needs of children and adolescents
- Facilitate the development and implementing of school- and classroom-based management, which maximizes student learning
- Address diversity by providing awareness and training
- Enable educators to provide challenging, developmentally appropriate curriculum that engage students in integrative ways of thinking and learning
- Prepare teachers to use research-based teaching strategies and to demonstrate high expectations for student learning
- Prepare teachers to use various forms of student assessment along with an ability to provide guidance and advice

Adopt a Whole-School Curriculum

Won't learners respond better when teachers use a variety of instructional approaches that make teaching and learning exciting. Emphasize teaching and learning strategies that have a meaningful context for students and are as active and applied as possible. Allow students to see how their learning in the classroom is connected to their lives and is valued by the community. Make use of community resources to enhance the curriculum.

Research says that the most successful schools are working on a curriculum-instruction program. Teachers must be aware of their achievement goals and become focused on linking learning across grades and between classes.

DESIGN FOR INNOVATIVE SCHOOLS

Most of these tips are becoming parts of the foundations of alternative schools across the nation and are providing the design for new innovative schools. These schools provide a successful academic learning program for students who come from a variety of backgrounds. These schools have designed highly ambitious programs that provide rich and challenging curriculum for all students; optimum working conditions for all staff; more effective use of time by students, teachers, and administrators; technology for an information age; and careful assessments that provide real accountability.

These innovative schools offer the following tips for success based on specific standards within their programs. These standards can be disseminated throughout other school programs. Many of our won't learners are successfully completing these programs.

Make Your School Student Centered

We must realize that children learn best when they are immersed in complex learning experience. Innovative alternative programs advocate

- Learner-centered education that improves the child's motivation to learn
- Evaluation of abilities, learning styles, and social contexts, which are important factors that affect the student
- Active learning where students discuss, research, and collaborate with one another and with the staff
- Student independence and decision making

In a student-centered school,

- Students best learn skills and concepts as tools to meet present demands rather than as facts to be memorized today in hopes of application tomorrow.
- Student welfare is top priority.
- Support networks are available to assist the students.
- Students are involved in student affairs.
- Learning is cooperative.
- Alternatives will be offered to meet the needs of the individual student.
- Constant modification of the curriculum is addressed and meets the needs of the students.

Develop an Individualized
Learning/Personalized Learning Program

Individualizing means that we personalize education by connecting the student's life to the learning in the classroom. When we allow children to make their own educational choices, studies found that they become more highly motivated, satisfied, fulfilled, and successful.

Many new schools

- Combine direct instruction with inquiry-based learning
- Believe children learn best if they are immersed in complex experiences and are given the opportunity to actively process what they have learned

- Travel different pathways to meet the same goals
- Encourage a personal relationship between teacher and learner
- Respect the unique way a learner perceives the world and then shape accordingly the way a child is going to learn
- Respect the learner as a person who is connected to a family, the community, and the larger world around him or her
- Are aware of individualized learning styles, including feeling and reflecting, reflecting and thinking, thinking and doing, and creating and acting

Create a Positive School Climate

Innovative schools believe that a positive school climate has the power to overcome risk factors in the lives of children. A positive school climate

- Engages students' minds and hearts
- Includes an atmosphere of support and encouragement
- Portrays warmth, acceptance, and respect
- Offers a sense of security and belonging
- Includes policies that encourage and permit individualized action
- Offers academically rich programs that address higher- as well as lower-order cognitive objectives
- Provides instruction that promotes student learning
- Removes the conflict between the student and the school
- Fosters creative problem solving, communication, cooperative learning, and informal dialogue
- Involves the parents and the community
- Includes self-initiated learning where teachers facilitate rather than direct
- Advocates for continuous evaluation

Classroom Environment Is Critical

One approach used in successful schools is constructivism, an approach to teaching based on research about how students learn. It is based on active, hands-on learning during which students are encouraged to think and explain their learning. Constructivism is based on the thinking of Dewey, Piaget, and Vygotsky.

These are the practices encouraged

- Teachers seek and value students' points of view.
- Lessons are structured to challenge students' suppositions.
- Staff members recognize that students must see relevance in the curriculum.
- Lessons are planned around innovative ideas.
- Student learning is assessed in the context of daily classroom investigation and learners control their own learning.
- New concepts are linked to something familiar, thus connecting what students already know to the new information.
- Teachers allow the students to experience, stress learning by doing through exploration, and encourage discovery and invention.

Additional strategies include

- Learning is active and cooperative.
- Cognitive dissonance is addressed and there is heavy use of analogies between historical events and current events (the slaughter of World War I compared to violence in urban America, for example).
- Policies that encourage and seek a win/win result are stressed. Win/win sees life as cooperative not competitive.
- Alternatives are stressed, choices are given.

The students are encouraged to

- Handle conflict appropriately.
- Be productive every day.
- Cooperate with staff.
- Think globally, act locally, and show respect for peers, staff, and parents.

Develop a Behavior Policy

A behavior policy needs to meet the social and emotional needs of the students. The key to preventing negative behavior lies in shaping children's beliefs, attitudes, and behaviors by advocating for student-centered choices and consequences as well as adult-centered environmental control.

In order to help our won't learners, schools must believe in establishing clear, objective limits and enforcing consequences.

- You cannot make students do anything they do not choose to do.
- By setting limits, you are offering choices. The student chooses the positive or the negative.
- You must be flexible if you want your limit setting to succeed.
- Place relationships before rules.
- Actively listen to the students.
- Enforce your consequences.
- Try and try again.

Enact a five-step approach to the limit-setting process.

1. Explain exactly which behavior is inappropriate.
2. Explain why the behavior is inappropriate.
3. Give reasonable choices and consequences. Stress the positive option.
4. Allow time. If you do not allow time, it may appear that you are giving an ultimatum.
5. Enforce the consequences.

Many schools also advocate listening and use the CARE model.

- C oncentrate: give your full attention.
- A cknowledge: use body language and facial expressions to let students know that you are listening. '
- R espond: Provide feedback.
- E mpathize: See options through the eyes of others.

Introduce Conflict Resolution

We are becoming increasingly more ethnically and culturally diverse. To protect the well-being of both majority and minority groups, people must get along with each other in school, at home, at work, and in the community.

At some schools, a peer counseling/mediation program that includes conflict resolution curriculum and training is in place. Core concepts include

- Defining the problem
- Summarizing and prioritizing root causes
- Identifying solutions
- Analyzing solutions
- Selecting the best solution and acting on it

When undertaking conflict resolution, these guidelines should be followed:

- Do not criticize one another.
- One person speaks at a time, the other listens.
- Allow time for discussion.
- Encourage ideas.
- Seek mutual understanding.

Know Thy Leaders

The role of the administrator is to develop the foundation for change and continued success. The administrator will

- Observe rituals and traditions that support the school's heart and soul
- Eloquently and passionately speak of the deeper mission of the school
- Celebrate accomplishments
- Act as model, potter, poet, actor, healer, historian, anthropologist, visionary, and dreamer

Administrators have developed the following "theories in action":

- Leaders confront chaos and challenge complacency.
- Leading is a shared endeavor and requires redistribution of power and authority.

- Effective leadership depends as much on character as on cognition.
- Take risks.
- Forge and create partnerships.
- Be accountable; accept responsibility.
- Embrace adversity. Conflict, contention, failure, and fear are the experiences that teach administrators to deal with adversity while maintaining respect and concern for others.
- Never quit. Go the distance.
- Reflect. Read, think, write, and share.
- Admit mistakes and fix them. Fixing solidifies credibility. It keeps one humble.
- Wait patiently, expectantly, and intensely for actions to have an effect, for reputation to grow, and for skills to sharpen.
- As with children, positive encouragement is a magic formula for parents, teachers, and all involved. The administrator who takes time to pat a teacher on the back or to dry the eyes of a frightened child is a most effective leader.
- Have fun. The school that plays together, stays together.

Parental Involvement Is a Critical Piece

Conventional wisdom says children are more likely to succeed in school when their parents are involved in their education. Parents are the school's best friends. Although it is important for parents to be represented on decision-making committees and involved in setting school direction, what parents most need and most want are closer connections to the learning process for their children. When parents are engaged and when students and their schoolwork are at the center of the conversation, teachers and parents can focus together on how children are learning. Both can offer observations about students' strategies, paces, and styles of learning; the ways they express what they know; and the kinds of teaching strategies effective for them. When teachers' insights are supported by parents' insights, teachers can more easily connect students' experiences to curriculum goals.

Encourage parent involvement.

- Cooperation and support from parents can lead to a positive climate in the classroom.
- The special efforts to open communication with parents may encourage them to take an active interest in their children's schoolwork and progress.
- Teachers can provide parents with strategies to increase the value of home reading. For example, talk to your child about characters and plots, ask them to make predictions or summarize stories.
- Encourage parents to serve as volunteers or tutors in the classroom.

The school can

- Encourage students and their families to come together for an hour of learning at the school several times a year.
- Build trust. Show parents a familiar, positive portrait of their child.
- Encourage parental engagement at home by helping with homework, discussing school activities, monitoring the child's time spent on homework and reading to the child and letting him or her read to the parent.
- Encourage parental engagement at school by volunteering, visiting, attending school events, and keeping the lines of communication open.

Encourage Community Service/Service Learning

Many school programs encourage all students to partake in service learning projects prior to graduation. The following show some advantages:

- Service learning is an instructional method that combines community service with a structured school-based opportunity for reflection about that service, emphasizing the connections between service experiences and academic learning.
- Service learning programs balance the students' need to learn with the recipients' need for service.
- Learners benefit by acquiring skill and knowledge, realize personal satisfaction, and accept civic responsibility.

- The community benefits by having a local need addressed.
- Projects based on experiential learning that begins with concrete experiences and ends in reflection can transfer knowledge and learning to new situations.

Service learning provides our best and most realistic starting point in the transformational process to sustain democracy, justice, and economic opportunity as we all learn to navigate the many social interactions required of effective citizens. Service learning is a key component in school programming. Students are provided with an opportunity to give back to their community while inspiring a sense of caring and compassion.

Encourage Community/Business Involvement

Community involvement is a dynamic process that encourages, supports, and provides opportunities for community members to work together to improve student learning.

Programs that take students out of school and into the community to volunteer, to learn about a career, or to study can be established anywhere, and they have proven to generate powerful results. Sometimes students find their vocational direction; sometimes they are able to help someone in need. Their intellectual growth can be significant. One result is inevitable: the community is brought together through new relationships between the generations. It becomes a kinder place to live, in which people of different ages, including our won't learners, come to know and trust each other.

Adults enjoy being mentors for teenagers, and teenagers blossom as role models for younger children. Teenagers are also a support system for the elderly. There is abundant anecdotal evidence suggesting that all of us, including young people, respond positively to interest and encouragement with an increased will to succeed.

Any school can grow when faculty, students, administrators, parents, and community members sit down together, discuss the future, and hammer out realistic goals for all involved.

We must learn to use our local resources, which may vary widely. Every community has businesses or individuals who want to contribute to a local foundation, which can support grants in the arts, for innovative teaching practices, or for a piece of equipment the school badly needs. Other local resources include hospitals, theaters, zoos, museums, and universities. These resources offer lectures, partnerships, and challenging learning experiences for students. In our imperfect world, let us learn from school/business partnerships that are succeeding.

School plus community equals an education that's more meaningful. Such ties are a way to make education more meaningful for students. The goal is to strengthen students' academic skills and interests by tapping into the resources of the community.

Local communities abound with collaboration. At the Houston, Minnesota, high school, students looked at business possibilities. Houston is on the popular Root River bike path, which has no bike facilities. So Houston became the first U.S. high school with a student-operated bike repair shop as part of its curriculum. At Okabena, Minnesota, site of the Heron Lake-Okabena secondary school, there was no food store or public exercise gym. So students interviewed local residents and identified needs; a convenience store was opened in the school and the gym was opened for community wellness. At many small communities across the nation, students' efforts produced walking trails, food shelters, playgrounds, tennis courts, and fulfilled other community needs. Student learning and community service go hand in hand.

Joe Nathan, founder and director of the Center for School Change at the University of Minnesota, says that lots of community service, while valuable, isn't tied closely to an educational curriculum in ways that expand learning and fail to appeal to the won't learners. For example, student visits to a nursing home are nice, but even better is an opportunity for young people to learn from the elderly about much earlier and vastly different eras, such as World War II, the pretelevision age, the American Indian Movement, and so on.

At one alternative school, students learned about Japanese relocation camps from a man who was born in San Francisco but placed in a West Coast camp during World War II when he was their age.

What about the blood spilled in the old Chicago market district when labor and business fought? Or the era when many cities were hotbeds of anti-Semitism? Or when Catholics could not get top political offices? Or when a famous criminal, John Dillinger, came to St. Paul, Minnesota?

What is important, says Joe Nathan, is that community history, society's changes, and people's experiences be linked to the educational curriculum. This requires greater collaboration between school and community. Such partnerships benefit both sides. The won't learners thrive when school/community collaboration exists.

Collaborations between schools and community-based organizations can help students develop lasting academic and life skills. Helping students change their futures is the focus. Student achievements can be of many different kinds—formal and informal, social and academic. From providing services for the elderly to rehabilitating an inner-city park, from performing in a children's theater to presenting proposals to community leaders—such achievements make a difference in each young person's course through adolescence and into the future. A significant number of young people not only have positive ideas about what the future holds but also have the knowledge and confidence to plan and reach their goals.

Won't learners emphasize the value of the life skills they have learned in a community-based program. Several said that participating in community service projects provided their first experience of being valued by adults. Students stressed how this regard fueled their self-confidence and changed their attitude toward personal dependability. One student, who took part in a community beautification program, said, "It gives me a sense of responsibility like when you have a job. . . . You've got to be there on time, work hard at it, get done what needs to be done. I've learned responsibility."

Parents, schools, and community members believe that these community-based programs help students "duck the bullet" of early pregnancies, drugs, street violence, and academic failure. These programs provide the sanctuary and support that enable young people to imagine a positive path and embark on it. Academics are boosted and life skills enhanced. What students experience outside of school is crucial to their success in school.

Students appreciate the benefits of substantive integration between the school and the community. A recent focus group in a San Francisco Bay area high school that serves a low-income, ethnically diverse community, said that the adults provided tutoring, computer use, and a safe environment, which helped students grow.

Activities organized around a central topic connect school instruction with real-life experiences in the community. In a theme-based program, students explore a concept through many lenses. Take the example of a nature theme. A nature walk was decided upon by a group of middle school students. One group sketched plants and trees; another recorded the sounds of nature; and a third group gathered pH samples from pond water. The group with the sketches compared their drawings to book illustrations and determined the names and origins of several plants and trees. The group who recorded sounds listened to a professional recording and discerned two distinct birdcalls. Students from the third group estimated the acid levels of their pond water samples. Each activity led to further activity in the community.

A well-defined, theme-based community program allows students to connect ideas, concepts, and experiences. "Cooking from many kitchens" led to sharing family recipes, which led to the realization that mathematics is a key concept in cooking. Cultural recipes led to a reflection on cultural identity, the history of food, and its relationship to culture and geography. New vocabulary was learned (sifting flour, separating eggs, pinching salt). Nutrition and healthy eating joined the focus. All this led to better communication with parents and the community. Authentic, meaningful experiences related directly to students' lives.

Volunteers from the community are also a great resource for a successful school program. In a time of dwindling resources, schools need to rely more on community support. When all the pieces come together, a volunteer in a school can produce dramatic results. One won't learner, when paired with a volunteer who gave her individual attention, maintained a better attitude and improved her behavior. "She is terrific. I can't believe this lady really cares about me . . . not just my reading skills but about me as a human being."

Successful schools believe that community involvement is a dynamic process that encourages, supports, and provides opportunities for community members to work together to improve student learning.

Involving the community in the operation of the school should be a top priority. The school is an integral part of the community. Bringing together diverse stakeholders, melding their resources, and stretching their minds to embrace new ideas are essential to school/community/ business involvement. By contributing to their community, youth begin to think of themselves as community members with a stake in what happens. Our goal then becomes one of developing partnerships, supporting students, and promoting active participation in addressing community issues and challenges.

Enrichment Programs

Create an after-school program that includes a rich mix of academics, recreation, and enrichment. It's 3 P.M. Do you know where your students/children are? One parent worries that his kindergarten child and his first grader are getting too "whacked" because they are away from home early morning until early evening. Is his children's after-school program a baby-sitting service that fills his kids' time meaninglessly? A mother, whose teenagers eat breakfast at a before-school program and stay for an after-school program, wants her kids to spend time wisely. She asks that her boys concentrate on homework during the program so she can use them for other things at home.

Parents worry about whether their children are safe and are using their time well. Several mention that their children are given the opportunity to take advantage of an art program staffed by a volunteer parent. This is a club that their kids enjoy. These parents are not as concerned about their children getting additional academic preparation after school as they are about their children being with caring adults.

With long commutes and extended working days for adults, some kind of after-school program has become a necessity for many families. The average family today has twenty-two fewer hours each week to spend at home than families had in the 1970s.

The so-called school day for most children rarely ends at 3 P.M. with kids traipsing home for milk and cookies. In addition, neighborhoods seem less safe, traffic is more congested, and fears about kids getting into trouble are more intense. The U.S. Census Bureau indicates that 6.9 million children (9 percent of the children ages five to eleven and 41 percent of children ages twelve to fourteen) regularly care for themselves without adult supervision.

These realities are changing the public's perceptions. Decisions about children's activities outside of school have long been a family matter. Nevertheless, a consensus is now emerging that schools share with parents the responsibility for providing programs and activities, safe places, and transportation to make out-of-school time productive for children and teens.

Faced with high-stakes testing, published results, and other high-pressure policies, many educators are now looking at how students spend the hours after school. After-school programs are emerging as a popular strategy for improving school performance. A well-designed program can lessen achievement gaps and deter such risky student behaviors as drug abuse and gang membership. This type of informal setting will also help establish closer and more comfortable ties between teachers and students. The teachers and students become an extended family. Many of our won't learners would probably have dropped out of school without the support and encouragement of their teachers.

After-school programs are relatively easy, as school reforms go. They do not require major changes in institutional structure or practice and they receive broad public support. In fact, growing evidence suggests that after-school program participation is associated with higher grades and test scores, especially for lower income students.

After-school programs can serve other important prevention and developmental functions. Educators realize that antisocial behaviors and social rejection can interfere with school achievement. There appears to be a link between after-school programs and lower involvement in risky behaviors, including a lower incidence of drinking, smoking, using drugs, having sex, and becoming involved in violence. There are also increased positive behaviors, such as better social and behavioral adjustments, better relations with peers, more effective conflict resolution strategies, and increased parent involvement. All students want to understand their personal experiences and to feel that they belong to society. After-school programs can play a special role in helping students realize these aspirations. A child who sees, discovers, and explores a situation gets the most out of it.

An after-school program can read like a parents' dream: Spanish lessons, chess club, creative cooking lessons, gymnastics, softball, baseball, plus homework tutoring.

Despite good intentions on the part of the schools, unless schools can support students' cultures while simultaneously providing access to required skills, young people are likely to see school as a place where success requires loss and even degeneration of one's family and community. Therefore, after-school programs must link the values, attitudes, and norms of students' cultural communities with those of the school culture.

After-school programs are an entry point for the development of community/school partnerships. Many alternative school programs expand and build on what children learn during the core school day. Students are given the opportunity to apply what they are learning in school and practice problem-solving skills in a variety of contexts.

Many schools offer tutorial services with an intense focus on reading and mathematics, activities that help increase and enhance study skills, and a Homework Club in response to the wishes of parents who recognize that many of their children live in environments where there is no place for them to find the quiet time that homework may demand. Students have access to computer-aided instruction, and service-learning projects are offered that include activities that support local senior citizens and build relationships with residents in the area around the school. Teachers in many schools offer weight training and team sports classes in martial arts. Finally, volunteers from the community can "adopt a kid." Students who are economically disadvantaged know little of the larger world. Trips to the library, a play or concert, museums, and other community events are part of an after-school program.

Whether schools should extend their primary duty—to educate students—to include offering after-school programs is still a matter of debate, but the connection between students' well-being and their capacity for learning suggests that the role of schools in providing after-school arrangements that are beneficial to the students will continue to grow.

As these programs multiply, we need more information about what works, how, and for whom. We need to know what outcomes are linked to what program models, and what approaches are most successful for students of varied ages, interests, needs, and backgrounds. After-school programs seem to be the latest silver bullet solution to social and educational challenges, but support will be short-lived unless programs meet expectations.

As public schools are called on more and more to meet the needs of the communities they serve, after-school programs are an important strategy. Providing students with opportunities to improve their academic skills while exploring their interests and newfound abilities helps them, their teachers, and their parents to build closer relationships. Connecting the schools with the community ensures that these all-too-often separate entities come together to address a common goal and to share in the responsibilities and successes.

Develop a Senior Support System

Senior support means un-retirement. This includes the fine art of making a second career your life's work.

Marv was teaching a group of inner-city kids how to fish at Cedar Lake when two of the kids took off running. Bewildered, Marv looked around for the cause of their fright, and saw two cows that had come down to the water for a drink. "They had never seen a cow before," Marv recalled with a smile, "and they didn't know how a cow would act."

It wasn't the first time Marv had to explain the bovine temperament, nor will it likely be the last. For several years, Marv has spent almost every day with kids from three elementary schools that partnership in a local environmental education program. "When I retired, I thought to myself, what could I do? I'm not going to sit around all day, so I might as well get out and do something. I love the outdoors and I love to fish and I wanted to share that with the kids."

Marv is not alone. In fact, he is part of a growing movement of retired professionals who are transforming what it means to grow older in America. Not content to embrace the "golden years" notion of leisure, recreation, and disengagement, the seventy-five-year-old Marv and others like him are looking for something different in later life. Liberated from the career ambitions and monetary pressures of midlife employment, they are embracing opportunities that promise greater meaning, stimulation, and the chance to make a difference in the lives of students.

For senior citizen volunteers in Marion County, Florida, reading to elementary school children leads to renewed support for public education. In recent years, migration trends among senior adults throughout the United States have transformed Sunshine State residents from young, middle-class families to a stratified population of elders. Many of these older adults have completed professional careers, have raised families, and are experts in the joys of grandparenthood. Now they seek a relaxed lifestyle and the opportunity to explore new interests.

The dynamics between the two generations are incredibly powerful. Many grandparent volunteers, whose own grandchildren often live far away, leave satisfied and renewed. The children, who often lack grandparent role models, benefit greatly from this experience with an older adult. A grandparent volunteer said, "Today, there are many single-parent families or fractured families without any grandparents. We are filling more than an academic gap."

The New Face of Retirement, a national survey of Americans ages fifty to seventy-five, conducted in late 1999 by Peter D. Hart Research Associates, shows clearly that if earlier work fed the body, men and women in their later years are now looking for ways to better serve the soul. The survey found that only 28 percent of Americans in this age-group view retirement in the old terms, as a time to take it easy and focus on recreation. Instead, 65 percent want to stay active, to take on new challenges, and to begin a new chapter in their lives. What better way than to work with our won't learners.

In our rapidly aging society, the support of older adults is critical for public education. Recognizing senior citizens as a rich, untapped resource, a handful of school districts have begun to implement systematic intergenerational programs.

Educators can scarcely afford to overlook age trends in the United States. The population of older Americans, which already reflects a sharp increase among citizens over eighty-five, will continue as the Baby Boomer generation reaches retirement age.

A critical piece in helping students is to encourage senior citizens to get close to growing children and teenagers if we are to restore a sense of community, knowledge of the past, and a sense of the future. The support of older adults is critical for public education. We must recognize senior citizens as a rich, untapped resource and promote active participation, which leads to structuring meaningful experiences. As we foster ongoing relationships using intergenerational programs, we can promote positive dynamics between the two generations, which leads to success for all involved.

The teachers interviewed offered the following strategies for success: Set up cooperative learning groups, not traditional groups; use a high percentage of group projects and a low percentage of oral questions and answers; and encourage manipulative devices and activities that allow feeling, touching, and freedom of movement. Many teachers also advocate for experience-based activities, peer tutoring, and cross-age teaching. Discussion revolves around interested topics related to current issues and a high rate of encouragement is offered. They send a message of caring, listening, and taking kids seriously.

So what do we know and what are we doing? We can summarize and conclude that the following strategies make a difference:

- *Early intervention.* Many children enter school far behind their peers, not knowing numbers and letters or that books are read from left to right and top to bottom. Many districts invest large sums of money annually to support community-based early intervention programs to increase the likelihood that students will arrive with the prerequisite skills for reading. Kindergarten Express is a program offered for students during the summer before they start kindergarten so that they enter the classroom better prepared.

- *Attendance.* The correlation between achievement and attendance is strong. Poor attendance is the first step toward dropping out. A major campaign has begun that focuses on improved attendance, involving the staff and community groups to create incentives for perfect attendance, recognizing and rewarding students and teachers with perfect attendance, and engaging families and community agencies.

- *Quality instruction.* A 1997 Commission of Education and America's Future report indicated that school success can be predicted primarily by three factors: family (49 percent), teaching quality (43 percent) and class size (8 percent). Because we can control 51 percent of the primary variables, investments in class size and quality instruction are essential to overcome family circumstances. Indeed, American public education has a long tradition of proving that there is no limit to a school's capacity to compensate for limited family resources.

- *Expectations of excellence.* We are not allowing the emphasis on basics to "dumb down" and narrow the curriculum. Active learning, inquiry, hands-on learning, and higher-order thinking skills must be part of the curriculum.

- *Good health.* Where did we ever get the crazy idea that to make kids *do* better, first we have to make them feel worse? Students *do* better when they *feel* better. Students need to come to school healthy and ready to learn. Students also need to be well rested. Many high schools start at 8:30 A.M. or 9:00 A.M. For the students who still have trouble functioning in the morning, an afternoon or early evening program is offered.

- *Consistency*. Many school districts have adopted a districtwide curriculum to account for high-mobility students.
- *Community support*. Community conversations in which leaders from the business, faith, and nonprofit worlds share ideas about behavior, safety, attendance, and assets for youth are crucial.
- *Multiple measures*. Accountability is not about a single test, on a single day, at one grade level. Tests may be useful but a single test does not provide a comprehensive picture of a student's knowledge, thinking, or understanding. Watching students in class, analyzing student work, observing student interaction, and seeing how they apply and transfer learning in new situations provides tremendous information about what works and what does not work.
- *Align curriculum, instruction, and assessment*. Any effort to improve achievement needs to align what we teach, how we deliver content and skills, and how we measure student performance.
- *Goals, feedback*. Three criteria (measurable goals, the use of feedback and performance data, and effective teamwork) are preconditions for environments where learning is the focus and continuous quality improvement is ubiquitous.

The challenge is not just to "restructure" and then settle into a repeating pattern of behavior. Schools must be able to continuously improve and recreate themselves by redefining the capabilities needed for success. Schools must not become like machines, but like living organisms, learning from their experiences. The skills, hopes, and dreams instilled by these learning environments will help the won't learners find confidence, hope, and opportunity on the educational playing field. Though the parents and children are from different cultures, religions, and communities, they all want the same things—safety, discipline, good morals, high academic standards, and a loving environment where their child is cared for as a person.

The public educational system must seek out reforms. It is about lives changed through the moral, social, and intellectual influence of a good school. We must use our many wonderful and dedicated teachers and parents to fight our large, impersonal, and bureaucratic school districts that often make reforms difficult, if not impossible, to implement. We must empower teachers and students to help make the climate one of learning, growth, and outreach—a place where students can build a bright future.

As we individually set up our plans and goals for creating successful schools, remember that we are in a different time span in which a new awakening has begun. Our life experiences and observations continuously mold us; what we do today, what we did in the past, and what we will do in the future give meaning to the present. Those discourses that disrupt are among the most powerful instruments of social change we can use today.

Michael Apple (1990) says that our task is to teach and to learn, to take our inquiries as seriously as the subject deserves, to take criticism of what we say respectfully and openly, and to hunger for it so that we, too, can be called upon to challenge and reformulate our own common-sense. Until we take seriously the extent to which education is caught up in the real world of shifting and unequal power relations, we will be living in a world divorced from reality. Let us rise to the task and teach to the individual and his or her learning style in schools that favor culture and individualism.

We are not finished. In our continuous-improvement community, our work is never done. Poverty, an influx of non–English-speaking students, and a more competitive marketplace challenge us today, and we will face new and different demands and expectations in the future. We are seeing impressive gains in achievement across all populations at all levels. We attribute this to the tips for success laid out in this chapter. Our community expects the best from us, and we expect to deliver exactly that.

7

SUCCESS STORIES

Just go out there and do what you've got to do.

—Martina Navratilova

Too many children are not prepared to meet the challenges they face in today's complicated world. Preparing youth requires giving them an effective education. The traditional three Rs (Readin', 'Riting and 'Rithmetic) are just the beginning. What is missing is the fourth R, Relevant skills. These skills, including communication, decision making, and goal setting, must be a part of all young people's basic education in order to cultivate motivated, goal-oriented, and community-minded individuals. When young people learn the fourth R, there is no limit to what they can achieve.

The successful alternative program focused on in this chapter was created in 1998 and is located in a colorful and diverse urban area. With almost 50,000 students, this urban district has students representing 100 languages and a wide range of ethnic groups (African American, American Indian, Hispanic, Asian American, Hmong, Somalian, Islamic, and white). As with many urban areas from 1980 to 2000, the percentage of non-Caucasian students increased from 31 percent to 71 percent and the percentage of students at the poverty level increased from 31 percent to 65 percent. Twenty percent of the students do not speak English as their native language, and that number is growing by about 1,000 students a year. This urban district has 127 schools, including 31 alternative schools, many of which have existed since 1980, and 8 charter schools that have opened since 1992. Entering kindergarten, students can choose from more than a dozen magnet and alternative schools; high school students have an array of magnet, alternative, and postsecondary enrollment options. School choice has been a fabric of this district since the early 1970s.

The focus of this alternative school is important to mention at this time because this school offers a chance to shed the mystery of alternative education and joins the challenge of educating all our schoolchildren in unprecedented ways. How this school came to be and how it works generates possibilities that can change the way we think about all our schools, rich and poor, rural and urban. It is a public school working in close collaboration with parents and the community under all the constraints of the public school system, but without all of the problems that plague so many schools today.

The student population is roughly equivalent to a cross-sampling of the district's learners. The majority of the students are African American and American Indian with a sprinkling of Hispanic and Hmong. Almost all students are low-income or poverty level and they experience a full range of academic strengths and weaknesses.

The doors opened in September 1998, with twelve students in grades four through eight and grew to seventy-six students in the course of the first year. When the twenty-four eighth-graders indicated that they did not want to leave and attend traditional high schools, a high school program was created. This ninth through twelfth-grade program opened in September 1999 with fifty-six students. It grew to 210 by June of 2000. By January 2001, there were 283 students and the population is continuously growing. More schools are under proposal and will be located in other areas of the district. This existing school is located five minutes south of the downtown metropolitan area.

The school is a place that successfully embodies a conception of education that challenges the low and trivial expectations found in most urban public schools. The school offers a rich and interesting culturally based curriculum full of powerful ideas and experiences aimed at inspiring the students' natural drive to make sense of the world around them, and trusts in the learners' capacity to have an impact upon it. The school is a haven where teachers "with the passion of the amateur and the competence of the professional" thrive, to quote David Ruenzel in an article on what African American parents are seeking from schools their children are attending (Urban Learners 2000).

For most of the staff and many of the parents, well-wishers, and friends, the success of the school is a dream come true. The parents are our first lines of defense. The school is surrounded by powerful outside friends like Joe Nathan, director of the Center for School Change, and Dr. Robert Brown, professor in the educational leadership department at the University of St. Thomas. The staff is filled with the heady vision that they can make a difference in the lives of the students, perhaps even in their lifetimes.

In many places in the United States, alternative schools are proliferating. During 1998–2000, a multitude of small schools that enroll high-school-age students opened across the country under various auspices. All involved some form of faculty and student choice prospects and far greater autonomy and self-governance than the American traditional public educational system had previously allowed. Some involved new partnerships with community groups. Several teachers and parents are beginning to think that they, too, can "create" their own schools. From the top to the bottom, the traditional educational system is readying itself for change.

The school began small and was carefully planned. The staff included veterans of experimental programs that had been destroyed by budgetary cuts and unsympathetic administrators, teachers who had been working in schools whose philosophies they strongly opposed, and a few colleagues fresh from student teaching. Most had experienced the fatigue that comes from cutting corners on the things that truly matter in order to meet the endlessly proliferating mandated programs and mandated accountability schemes. All the staff has a passion to work with and give back to students in a child-centered, community-centered environment. They personalize and remember that diversity among people strengthens the larger community. The subject matter is looked at as "powerful stuff" that makes up our common world. The new is rooted within the old. The staff looks for strengths within traditions. Intellectual toughness of teachers, not just of kids, is demanded; above all, the teachers, parents, and business partners advocate for the students.

A typical classroom is not stacked with photocopied fill-in work sheets, but is literally full of stuff: books of every sort, paints as well as paintings, computers, plants, animals, fish, broken computers to repair or at least remove useable parts from, things. The curriculum is both conceptual and tangible. Students are falling in love with stories of the past, including their own. The staff is caring, open, friendly, and committed. The staff listens with a critical ear to what is said to parents, wondering how the message would be heard through a parent's ears.

This school is not meant to be replicated piece by piece. If what is being done is to have wider applicability, there is a need to look upon the story as an example, not a model, and then make it easier, not harder, for interested parties to do similar things in their own way. There is not just one correct, perfectly crafted, expertly designed solution. Good schools, like good families, good communities, and good societies, celebrate and cherish diversity.

With this introduction, let us now walk in the footsteps of our won't learners as we celebrate their success stories. Their names have been changed; their stories are true.

Roy: An Important Contributor

We struggled with how to teach Roy. He expressed enthusiasm in disruptive ways, such as being excessively talkative. Some of his manic activity appeared to be out of his own control. Roy had great difficulty with reading and writing. We worked with him outside the building, on the front steps, or on a walk to the river. We read the words and sentences he could not decipher so he would gain confidence. He soon was eager to read to us. Back in the classroom, we gave Roy roles that he could improvise rather than read. His best moment was when he played the role of Puck in Shakespeare's *A Midsummer Night's Dream*. The class explained that Puck was tormenting the lovers in the woods. Roy deftly interacted with the students who were reading their parts, usually in a sure way to antagonize. Roy experienced success.

Writing came next. Roy's spelling was erratic and his handwriting was poor. After much experimentation, I came up with a solution that allowed Roy to dictate to me. I typed Roy's words, verbatim, including expletives and wandering thoughts. Roy reviewed for errors and made corrections. We moved to where I dictated to Roy and he would fill in the blanks. By the end of the school year, Roy wrote an article for the school paper. He advised eighth graders about what to expect in ninth grade. It was a funny article and included serious as well as lighthearted advice. Roy's peers consider him an important contributor to the class.

Shayma: A Changed Person

Shayma was not sociable with the other students and had a reputation of wanting to be left alone. She often would sit in front of a computer screen all day, unwilling to either hold a conversation with staff or peers or look anyone in the eye. She refused to complete daily class assignments. We encouraged her, greeted her at the door when she arrived, complimented her on her hair and clothes, and always asked how she was doing. She responded with sullen looks, mumbles, and downcast eyes. We persisted; she resisted. Gradually, Shayma started to come into my office. She would ask for paper or a pencil when it was clear that she had these items. She made feeble attempts at conversation. I always responded. Soon this became a daily ritual. I asked the staff to stop in when they noticed Shayma in my office. She responded to them as well. She became more sociable with adults; two weeks later, she spread this newly discovered sociability to a few peers. Her newfound confidence was striking. Shayma became a changed person.

Sunny: A Late Bloomer

Sunny is an American Indian ninth-grader who carries a diagnosis of Fetal Alcohol Syndrome (F.A.S.). He was one of our original twelve students when the school was first opened. His foster mother requested that he become part of the program in September 1998 when his former school social worker recommended that he be placed in a residential special education site. Mom refused to believe that he was incapable of learning, even though she had been told this for years. She also harbored a deep distrust of the traditional school system. She had heard about the newly created school and called to see if her son could enroll.

Since enrolling, Sunny has expanded his math and reading skills. Beating all odds, Sunny passed the state-required Basic Standards Math and Reading tests required for high school graduation. "I love this school and you, Darlene, and all the teachers love me," says a proud young man. Sunny's foster mother simply said, "Thank you for taking my son and believing he could do it. You saved him from a world of darkness." Sunny's foster mother died suffering from cancer in February 2000, knowing Sunny was thriving in a world of love.

Jill Learns from Words

Jill has good verbal skills, uses vivid imagination, and concentrates well. Reading comes easily and she writes her own summaries of what she has read to enhance her comprehension. Math is more difficult since Jill needs verbal explanations. To cement her understanding of the concepts, we encourage her to describe how she solves her problems. She is a successful learner when allowed to proceed in this manner.

Liz Learns from Images

Liz has weak verbal skills and prefers visualizing, recognizes patterns, and pays attention to details. Reading can overwhelm Liz; therefore, we encourage her to read using a highlighter to emphasize the main points of the text. Because she learns visually, explanations are not enough. In mathematics, Liz studies examples of solved problems to figure out concepts.

Jill and Liz are success stories of how one small school personalizes education in order to help the learner become more highly motivated, fulfilled, and successful. Jill and Liz are two examples of what small schools can do to enhance learning.

Sherita: A Lost Soul

Sherita was a C−/D− student at her previous school. Rarely in trouble and even more rarely involved, Sherita moved from class to class, touching nothing. Sherita had become a high school specter in reverse; her body was physically present, her spirit was lost. Sherita had received an average of twenty negative messages a day from her previous school:

"You're late." "You forgot your homework." "You failed the test." "You don't know the answer." She was also described with a series of negatives: "Sherita is at risk." "She is not gifted." "She doesn't set goals for herself." "She won't learn." Sherita caused no problems, so she received very little attention. She was referred to this school because she was more than a year behind in credits for graduation. Since joining the program, Sherita has thrived in an atmosphere of support and encouragement. We encouraged and valued her points of view and stressed the positive. A personal relationship was quickly developed between Sherita and the teachers. She became motivated and her spring report card showed a B average.

Bianca: Shy and Retiring

Bianca was afraid to speak up in class. She hated going out for recess because the other children made fun of her poor reading skills. She and her mother floundered nightly over her homework. This school helped turn Bianca into a confident, happy, and successful sixth grader. We looked at what learning issues Bianca was facing. We assessed strengths and weaknesses. Skill gaps were pinpointed and we came up with a blueprint for an individualized program to fill in the gaps and helped Bianca meet her specific learning needs. She was allowed to progress at her own pace and she received personal attention for optimal learning. With love and caring, Bianca soon was able to demonstrate mastery of academic skills. Her math and reading skills increased one full grade level in only five months. Self-esteem also soared. Bianca is still quiet but once in a while you will hear her shout out an answer with confidence.

Sam: A Future Leader

Sam is a tenth-grade African American student who was also one of the original twelve students enrolled at the school. Sam's parents chose to enroll him because he was having difficulty at a charter school he had been attending. Since joining our program, Sam's grades are in the A/B range and he exhibits zero negative behaviors. Sam became the student body president and has become the official student spokesperson for the school at community events and business luncheons. Sam says, "This school has the best teachers and principal I have ever been with. You all listen and work one-on-one with me. You help me with learning the skills I need to be a future leader." Sam's parents are amazed at the transformation. Sam Sr. says, "You have saved my son from the road leading to dropping out. When I walk into this high school, I feel the love."

Marlon: A Suspense Story

Marlon is a very active child who was referred to the school by a nearby elementary school. As a fourth grader, Marlon was unable to read or write and had been constantly suspended for negative behavior. He would use inappropriate language, run out of the classroom and the building, and expect the staff to chase him down the street, which we did for safety reasons. Marlon was also establishing a pattern of skipping school and was already involved with the court system because of truancy issues. At this school, Marlon enchanted us with his smile and twinkling eyes. He responded positively to our atmosphere of caring and love. He quickly learned to read and write, negative behavior lessened, and his attendance is close to being perfect. "Everyone likes me, even if I am bad," says Marlon. "They let me be me." Marlon's mother says that this school has worked miracles for her son. "He never wants to miss school, even if he is sick. I can't thank the staff enough for caring. The other schools had already given up on him." Marlon, now a sixth grader, is in his third year with the program.

William, Who Won't Give Up

William is a clown and a goof-off. However, character-wise, he is beyond reproach. Honesty and integrity are part of his character. He is caring, compassionate, and makes pretty good choices in most settings. He is also prone to acting on impulse. Will attended several different public schools before being transferred to this program. Will and I have butted heads on several occasions. Through it all, I believed in him and he kept coming back. "I'm a person who can't stand not knowing the right answer and I don't like to be wrong and I can't give up on things

that I try to accomplish. I won't let myself give up . . . that's my motto
. . . live life to the fullest and you have nothing to worry about. I make
no promises, but I'll try."

Miguel: Aggressive No Longer

Miguel was a shy and withdrawn child (sixth grade) who spoke very
little English and who appeared to stutter when he spoke his native
Spanish. His Spanish reading and writing skills were very low. Although
math is a strength, his previous teachers did not seem to notice. (Grades
from his previous school showed D/F.) Recently arrived from a small
community in southern Mexico, Miguel lived with more than fourteen
relatives (nine adults and five children) in a two-bedroom apartment.
He often came to school hungry and tired, wearing dirty clothes.
Shunned by his former classmates, Miguel became belligerent and aggressive. Miguel was referred to the program after he displayed severe
aggression toward a female teacher.

We assigned Miguel to a male teacher who spoke very limited
Spanish. A bond was formed and Miguel started trying to please the
teacher. He would do anything for him. We also involved a high
school Spanish-speaking young man to act as a big brother to Miguel.
We stressed the positive and discovered Miguel had an incredible talent for drawing. We used this talent to enhance his reading and writing skills. Printing letters became an art project. His classmates offered to help him learn English. An eighth grader worked patiently to
help Miguel learn to read better. Miguel was able to return the favor
by helping others in mathematics. Miguel has shown no aggressive actions in weeks, is speaking and reading English, and my office is dec-
orated with many of his drawings.

The above are examples of service learning, where students learn to
recognize both their responsibility and their power to create social
change. This has been a valuable and important area in our curriculum
that causes our won't learners to be "doing well and doing good."

Part of the mission of the school is to develop students who will succeed and do well. The teachers have a vision of social justice, equity, and
the possibility of a better world that is transmitted to the students.

One of our won't learners, Travis, agreed to work as a tutor in a kindergarten class at a nearby elementary school. Travis is really a big guy. On the first day in that classroom, he broke the little chair that he sat in; from that moment on, the little kids adored him. To them, he was a big cuddly bear. They hugged him all the time, around the knees, which was as high as they could reach. He became a big brother in their lives. Travis accepted his role and the responsibility it entailed. Because of his new role, his attitude toward school and learning changed. This young man learned that the "learning" part is directly related to the "service" component. He also learned community connections and the reciprocity between the server and the group being served. "One of the first things I learned is that you get back more than you can ever dream of giving," says Travis with a big grin.

Many students find meaning through opportunities to contribute to their world. Listen to Toua:

> When I go over to the nearby elementary school to tutor two Hmong-speaking second graders, they are excited to see me. I guess they don't get much attention from a teacher and a classroom that is strictly English speaking. When I am with them, I feel special. I am an average student at the high school. I'm not a physical person. I'm not great looking and don't stand out in any way. I guess that's okay with me. I am okay because two hours each week these two little kids make me feel like I am the most important person in the world. It's been great for all of us because now the entire class wants to learn Hmong. We are counting and learning simple phrases. I've been given a chance to share my heritage, language, and culture with little kids. This makes me proud.

This won't learner was given a community service project that gave him an experience of contributing real value to his community. Giving students the chance to discover how to match their particular passions to the needs of others gives meaning and purpose to one's life. Toua now wants to learn.

Many of the families that were interviewed said that they noticed improvements in the behavior and attitude of their children after they started attending the school. Parents indicated that their children read more, were happier about attending school, earned better grades, and did not get into as much trouble.

One seventh-grader in the program wrote the following in response to a journal assignment. When asked to respond to the question, "How has this school affected you?" the student wrote,

> I didn't know how to read. I said to myself, how could I do my work if I can't read? I was ashamed to ask for help. At my other school, the teachers said that if I wasn't so lazy I could learn to read. I was getting all Fs on my report card. My Mom was very disappointed in me and mad at me. So I said why come to school and I missed over half the school year. I was kicked out of my first school and told to go someplace else. I started going here and the teachers were great. They helped me one-to-one and on the computer, especially LaMar. So I kept coming to school and did my work. Then I knew my life was changing. I could read better. Now I am not ashamed to read in my classes. My grades are better. My Mom is impressed with how I changed. Now I even get rewards in all my classes.

Many of the students were eager to be quoted. The following comments were made by won't learners who were asked to leave their home schools because of lack of credits for graduation and/or poor attendance records. They are proud of what they said and asked that their names be used. The question was simply, what do you think of our school?

Cory: "The teachers help me and correct me without making me feel ashamed or stupid. I don't get picked on anymore. I will succeed."

Sherice: "Teachers help us one at a time so we understand better. Alternative schools help you get an education while you help yourself."

Cortez: "I get a chance to show my talents and maybe succeed. You all give me a chance to do my own work at my pace."

Darnell: "This is a great school because it allowed me to have a second chance. Without these types of schools, a lot of students would drop out. When you mess up in public schools, that's bad enough, but not having anywhere to go is even worse. I am taking advantage of my second chance. I've learned a lesson about responsibility and will handle my business after I leave here."

Christine: "If you are really trying to get an education, you need to want that education for you. Then you can get the help you need."

Alex: "Alternative schools are second chances to get what is right for us."

Maria: "In this school, kids have more freedom than in a regular school. I like that. I am comfortable because I know that I have time to finish my work."

D'Angela: "I am getting my goals accomplished on a daily basis. When I get to school, I sit down, do my work, and don't get up until I am done. When I am finished, I use the Internet for further research or read the newspaper. I stay engaged."

Quanee: "This school helps me learn and focus. I can get the help I need. I don't fit in the other schools so I need this one."

Dale: "I don't really need help with learning. I just need to start applying my skills more to take advantage of what life can offer."

Antasia: "All I need to learn is an assignment, pen and paper, and maybe a little explaining, and I am on my way."

Ali Jama: "I really appreciate what you all have done for me. Thank you."

Ebony: "I have to work to help support my family. You allow me to leave early to get to my job and still keep up with my homework."

Eddie: "My biggest problem at my old school was skipping classes at lot. The teachers were boring. They talked the whole period and gave you two minutes to work. Here I get my work, do it, and any questions I have I just ask. I haven't missed a day since I started."

Richard: "It's easier to study here because you have the time for it. You are not rushed into anything. It's not crowded like a regular high school so you can concentrate much better. We are treated better instead of being dogged. I need a school like this."

Elijah: "Alternative schools are really cool but this one is really tight because of the teachers. They help and really care about me inside and outside of school."

Korey: "Thinking about how far behind in credits I was, I had to do something about my situation. This school is giving me a second chance to better myself. I can study things differently and deeper than at other schools."

Meko: "Fewer students mean the teachers have more time to help me. Most schools it seems the teachers were too busy to help me. Now I can see graduation is possible for me."

Dwight: "Alternative schools like this one help get you back on your feet."

John: "You understand that kids have lives outside of school. You don't judge us because we have different lifestyles. The teachers here really care about me succeeding. I don't have an attitude toward teachers anymore."

Aries: "I can have an opinion without getting into trouble."

A.M.: "Learning is all about the mind and the teachers let me develop and use my mind."

Wia: "I learned to accept myself for who I am."

This is our school. The school was created to ensure that the students have a successful school experience by giving them the skills that they need to become responsible adolescents and young adults. We urge our students to take responsibility for their learning in a climate that is culturally relevant and that uses a holistic approach to teaching and learning. The school enrolls students who will benefit from a small school environment and offers hands-on learning for those students who do not respond to traditional methods.

This school and many others like it have increased student achievement for youth in the inner city by providing at-risk students with the opportunity to become the *best that they can be*. These schools empower students to become independent, respectful, and productive members of their communities. Our mission statement, which says *each student will achieve to her/his fullest potential in a learner friendly environment*, is being achieved.

Joe Nathan says it best, "Many people talk about what is wrong in education today. This school is an example of what is right."

The young people quoted in this chapter are firmly on the path to becoming contributing members of society. They have great potential, great energy, and great dreams. They represent our nation's most valuable resource. Their lives with all of their wonderful possibilities are the fruits of educating the human will.

To quote Ralph Moore: "The REAL credit in life should go to those who get into the ARENA. If they fail, they at least fail while DARING TO BE GREAT. Their place in life will never be with those COLD AND TIMID SOULS who know neither victory nor defeat" (Clark 1999).

8

WHERE DO WE GO FROM HERE?

We are still not where we are going, but we are still not where we were.

—Natasha Josefowitz

Thanks a lot.

Darlene, Cathy, LaMar, Naila, Ann, Bruce, Phil, Jock, and Greg, too. This is a little something to show my appreciation.

Me liking school never crossed my imagination. You guys just don't know how you got me infatuated with the thought of graduation. Before I came to this school, I never thought I'd finish school because hanging out and smoking weed was all I wanted to do. But y'all helped me change my mind about school by showing me that y'all really cared. You helped me through my tough times by being there. When I graduate y'all be the same people that I will thank for helping me to be able to say KISS MY ASS to the people who said I COULDN'T, I WOULDN'T, and AIN'T GONNA.

Thanks,

From Montwanique Terry
Class of 2002

American schools are in trouble and inner-city students, including our won't learners, suffer the most. Despite ever-increasing funding for education, test scores have been falling since 1963, and today it is virtually impossible to get a decent education in many inner-city schools. There are, however, a few rays of hope, from research on what makes a good school to structural reforms that give our won't learners access to these schools. This chapter focuses on strategies to help those who work with our won't learners encourage schools to provide the support they need.

We are at risk of losing an entire generation of students to the culture of poverty. Schools must be accountable to students, parents, and teachers, not to bureaucrats, politicians, and interest groups. We have a system with problems. We need to seek radically different alternatives. We must return quality education to American classrooms, and heed the words of Henry Miller: "Any genuine philosophy leads to action and from action back again to wonder, to the enduring fact of mystery." It is imperative that we heal the wounds of division in our educational system and reach out to the mystery of the won't learners.

Are we living in days when hope is a rare commodity and idealism is a lost art? Perhaps we have grown traumatized by the daily tragedies in our world—ethnic cleansing, religious bigotry, neo-Nazism, anti-Semitism, terrorism (acts leading to the collapse of New York's World Trade Center and the destruction at the Pentagon), sexual harassment, entrenched racism, brutal acts of violence (Columbine, and Los Angeles high schools)—and feel powerless as they focus on day-to-day survival.

Each one of us must become an artisan of change, highly skilled at a craft and committed to excelling at this proficiency. Artisans of change are individuals whose visions emerge from experiences with won't learners. They are also activists who design and implement methods for moving from the way things are to how things should be.

A fresh vision of community needs to emerge if we are to enforce change. This means removing ineffective educational systems so brand new approaches can originate. We must continually evaluate our educational system. If the current system does not work, something needs to change.

New understanding cannot be contained by old structures. A fresh approach to community entails new methods and skills, new tools. We must listen to all voices and allow sharing to take place. In order to create an environment where everybody's voice is heard, we will need to become skilled at what James Earl Massey calls the "discipline of dialogue." Massey describes it this way: "Dialogue is the personal dimension of sharing. It is the self-conscious response of an individual with another self. Dialogue is the way of explored intention."

In order to allow values of equality to develop, we must take others seriously as persons. Therefore, we must develop the art of listening. While listening, we must become open. Openness must be indicative of the school's philosophy of education; staff is open to new curricula, new ideas, and new ways to solve problems. Staff is willing to take risks. An open attitude pays off in terms of student success.

If we are to practice the discipline of dialogue in regards to educational reform, we must become fluent in cultures other than our own. The widespread effects of racism require us to work through stereotypes and develop sensitivity to cultural difference. This is particularly true for those who are isolated in urban settings. It is imperative that all of us become adept at understanding differences. We may never become "experts" on the lives of others, but we can become "fluent" in a variety of cultures and learning styles. We must allow ourselves to see the world through the eyes of the won't learners, and allow life experiences to mold our way of perceiving and thinking.

"He motivated us by engaging us in activities that we loved, and he got us out of our seats and involved in learning in ways that were meaningful to each of us." (Quote by a won't learner admiring Bruce, a social studies teacher)

In this age of diversity, when many urban learners are poor, feel oppressed, and experience prejudice based on race, culture, gender, skin color, or social status, we must take up again the most urgent question: Can educational reform become liberating? Can change lead to liberation and justice at a societal and structural level? Is educational reform a source of empowerment for educators, cultures, and the won't learners?

In the early 1970s, Jerome Bruner wrote that education is in a state of constant invention. Each generation must define afresh the nature, direction, and arms of education for the sake of the new generation. We have not taken his advice; as a result, we have ended up with bureaucratic structures and big autonomous schools that do not meet the needs of the majority of today's students.

We can look for a common denominator when looking at schools working with won't learners. Each school knows that it is responsible for improving student achievement. The schools focus on what needs to be done in order to increase achievement. They do not make excuses. They do not ignore the problems that children bring to school with them, but they look for and generally include ways to engage students, to encourage, incite, and inspire them. Theories, political battles, and legislation are interesting pieces in the educational program, but what matters most in education is what happens to young people day to day.

The goal is to transform schools into an organization focused on the academic task with a method of getting there. It can't be done by a mandate. It has to be done one school at a time.

Blending academic knowledge, demonstrated performance, and real-world experience is the way to reach the won't learners and any disadvantaged, disengaged students. "If you give them a real job, they are going to perform for you," says Johnny Smith, director and co-chair of the board at Heart of the Earth Charter School, an American Indian charter school in Minneapolis, Minnesota.

Politics, patronage, funding, and fear are a few of the barriers that we must overcome on our journey to improving schools. Large numbers of children are coming to school not ready to learn.

Is our system perfect? No way! But we (teachers and administrators at schools across the United States) are working on ways to better integrate our classrooms and raise student achievement.

Evidence has grown steadily in the last several years that reduced class sizes, in particular, can have a dramatic and long-lasting effect on student achievement, especially with children of poverty. Reducing class size gives every student more of the teacher's time and more individual attention in order to grasp the academic material to meet high standards.

How have schools focused on student achievement?

Atlanta public schools implemented a new educational reform initiative in 2000 beginning in ten schools. Baltimore City public school residents get a head start on learning because the district offers a full-day prekindergarten in eleven elementary schools.

Broward County (Florida), the nation's fifth-largest school district, implements the Character Education Initiative, eight character traits integrated into the curriculum and taught to all students. The character traits taught are responsibility, citizenship, kindness, respect, honesty, self-control, tolerance, and cooperation.

California's Long Beach Unified School District launched a new K–12 character education curriculum to teach common values such as caring, citizenship, justice, fairness, and respect to make sure students have a clear understanding of the difference between positive and negative behavior.

Charlotte-Mecklenburg, North Carolina, has teamed with several communities and corporate organizations to provide students with greater access to technology within their neighborhoods. The Computer Access to Neighborhoods (CAN) offers one-on-one tutorial for eighth and twelfth grade students who have not met North Carolina computer skills proficiency requirements. Students are able to access tutors and computers in more than twenty-five community locations, including area churches, recreation centers, and YMCAs. Corporate volunteers tutor students after school and on Saturday mornings.

Denver public schools have launched a five-high-school program in which students may earn a high school diploma and also earn one year of community college credit.

The District of Columbia public schools have launched a "Passport" program for middle school students to learn outside of schools. Students will be given passports to museums, monuments, embassies, and other points of interest.

Houston, the nation's seventh-largest school district, has devised an innovative way to combat teacher shortage by using the Internet to educate and certify teachers.

Miami-Dade County (Florida) introduced an initiative to strengthen math and science education. They incorporated material from NASA and other space programs.

Milwaukee public schools opened the 2000 school year with lower class sizes in kindergarten through third grade classes in eighty-eight schools as a result of the SAGE program (Student Achievement Guarantee in Education).

A new attendance policy went into effect in the Minneapolis public schools that requires students to attend school at least 95 percent of the school year, missing no more than eight days. The policy details circumstances for excused absences, but also sets consequences for secondary students who have more than four unexcused absences from a class a semester. These students risk failing the class. (This is well and good on paper, but I challenge Minneapolis to set plans in action that will inspire our won't learners and all others to want to attend school. Students who want to learn will not have an attendance problem.)

Virginia's Norfolk public schools have developed a program with Tidewater Community College to prevent students who are older than their classmates from dropping out of school. The Best-Key Alternative Training Program offers students training on the college campus, assessments to determine gaps in basic academic skills, and technology, job-readiness, and life-skills education.

California's Sacramento School District expanded its "home visit" program (in which teachers visit students in their homes) to the district high schools. The program was developed in 1998 to help parents gain the knowledge and skills necessary to become more active participants in their children's education.

The roles and models presented by these schools can be disseminated to interested schools and districts across the country. Each can help us decide where to go from here.

Raising children isn't easy, as we all know. The task becomes even more difficult when we do not give kids the education they deserve. We send them off to school every day, hoping for the best but often settling for less. Teachers are usually overworked and underpaid. Public schools are often overcrowded and underfunded. We begrudge tax hikes for education, and then bemoan low test scores.

There has been more and more evidence of extensive high school failure and inadequacy. At the same time, our educational system remains steady in its resistance to change. Its size, fragmented units and programs, specialized personnel, and hierarchical organization combine to make secondary education firmly resistant to reform and improvement measures.

Both internal and external critics have pointed out the shortcomings of our educational system, especially the large high schools. The latter have offered dramatic accounts of the neglect and chaos in inner-city schools. These urban schools are responsible for effectively serving an increasingly culturally diverse and economically heterogeneous student population. These schools are challenged to address issues of program specialization and social integration. It is estimated that over 25 percent of the student population in the nation's elementary and secondary schools will be from socially, culturally, and linguistically diverse backgrounds by 2005.

The United States was founded as a nation intended to absorb people from other nations. However, the melting pot concept does not diminish one's heritage. It unites the strengths of many cultures into a single, stronger blend of culture to reflect the best of all.

In just over two hundred years, this country became the greatest nation on earth. We've had more Nobel Prize recipients than any other industrialized nation. We've sent men into outer space and brought them back alive; we've pioneered open-heart surgery, and our science and technology are copied worldwide. Those who accomplished these incredible feats were the products of an educational system that emphasized academics.

But at the same time, for almost twenty years, critics of education have concluded that boredom is epidemic within classrooms; even in "good" schools, students are only superficially engaged in what they do. In several schools, as many as two-thirds of the students have simply disengaged or tuned out on academic learning. Also, in a large number of classrooms, tacit agreements between teachers and students stipulate that teachers will not demand very much; in return, the students will not get out of hand.

We cannot think this way. We must place the student first. We must match the diversity of the student with a diversity of opportunities for both students and their teachers. Let's create classrooms where teachers have abandoned the traditional role of "teacher talk" to become "classroom coaches" who guide students as they discover knowledge.

How far are you willing to go?

Redefining public education, Ravitch and Viteritti suggested in 1997, will involve three educational models: new contracting arrangements, charter and alternative schools, and school choice. Americans are clamoring for these choices as we move toward educational reform that will place the student first. More and more parents want to send their children to schools that offer individualized programs, culturally based curriculum, intensive phonics, or cutting-edge technology. They want results. This means equipping their son or daughter with skills to cope in today's society.

At the same time, educators complain that state and federal rules and regulations are squelching experimentation. How can schools improve when they are bound in bureaucracy? How can they guarantee results when they see their programs tangled in red tape?

It is at the intersection of these demands (more choice, more accountability, and less red tape) that the charter school idea emerged. The concept is simple: Swapping rules and regulations for results. These schools pursue innovative teaching methods that will enhance student learning styles and improve student performance.

The won't learners find school extremely difficult, especially reading and writing. However, these same students are very capable of successful learning in the world outside school. The same student who didn't seem able to learn the simplest concepts associated with reading, writing, spelling, or math showed evidence of being able to learn and apply much more complex knowledge and skill in the everyday world. These kids have street smarts and can passionately argue an issue they care about.

The innovative teachers that were interviewed, similar to other teachers found in alternative educational settings, summarized:

- Learning is a process of habit formation.
- Students are more likely to learn if they believe that the learning experience has value, purpose, and use for their lives.
- Students are more likely to engage when associated with someone they like, respect, admire, trust, and would like to emulate.

Students who attend alternative settings are doing so for a variety of reasons. Some are mandated by law to be there; others are deficient in credits to graduate for medical, truancy, or behavioral reasons. Some have learning disabilities, and others simply thrive academically and socially in a nontraditional learning environment.

We must teach these learners to be *proactive*, to cultivate a mind-set of proactivity. This means taking the initiative, not waiting for others to act first, and being responsible for what you do. Keep in mind that there are three central values in life: the experiential (that which happens to us), the creative (that which we bring into existence), and the attitudinal (our response to difficult circumstances). We have the initiative and the responsibility to make things happen.

Our teachers need to *begin with the end in mind*. This involves the ability to visualize and project into the future the consequences of our actions today. Many of our students exhibit no sense of hope for the future—academically, financially, or socially. When we encourage students to begin with the end in mind and to create a lifework plan, they then have a personal decision to guide their daily activities.

Third, *put first things first*. Students in alternative settings, our won't learners, often exhibit an inability to prioritize or organize. We need to reinforce that it is critical to learn to delay immediate gratification through inappropriate sexual behavior or drug use. We need students to answer the question: What one thing could you do in your personal life that, if you did on a regular basis, would make a tremendous positive difference in your life?

Fourth, *think win/win*. This addresses the need for many of our students to resolve conflict nonviolently. Developing peaceful, empowering negotiation skills are critical for learners who have often been combatant, violent, engaged in gang activity, or enveloped in familial relationships where the presence of alcohol and drug addiction made communication impossible on anything but an abusive, demeaning, argumentative level. In many of these students' families, it is unlikely that they have seldom, if ever, experienced win/win.

Teaching students to communicate for win/win is an integral lifelong skill for participating in a peaceful global society. Win/win is also an appropriate choice in situations where personal ethics, values, or their moral frameworks are in danger of being compromised.

Fifth, our learners need to *see models of empathetic listening skills, which are built on openness and trust*. Empathetic listening is listening with intent to understand the other person's frame of reference and feelings. There is often little or no opportunity for our students to engage in positive query with family members who are often under the influence of alcohol or drugs, too angry, defensive, guilty, or afraid to be influenced. We must teach our students to listen with their ears, eyes, and hearts.

Students may also come from home environments that are not conducive to collaboration and empowerment. Therefore, we need to provide our students with a sixth habit, *opportunities to connect to the community*. This connection can be through experiential learning, volunteerism, or mentoring relationships. We can also assist our learners to identify their personal inner gifts and strengths, which enrich group projects and relationships.

Finally, we need to *encourage our learners to take personal responsibility for their physical, emotional, and social health.* Many of our won't learners have not experienced a joyful, playful childhood. We need to encourage these students to rediscover their childlike nature, to engage in healthy playfulness, to discover the pleasures in giving to others and engaging in community service, to develop healthy eating habits, to exercise routinely, and to smile often. (The above suggestions are based on Stephen Covey's *Seven Habits of Highly Effective People* and adapted for students in alternative schools.)

Where do we go from here? We must create partnerships between schools and families. Sharing the responsibility for a child's education should be part of the solution to many of the social and economic problems facing our society today.

Education in the United States is not a single, uniform system that is available to every child in the same way. Children of different social classes are likely to attend different types of schools, to receive different types of instruction, to study different curricula, and to leave school at different rates and times. Jack Mezirow (Ravitch and Viteritti 1997) says that a defining condition of being human is that we have to understand the meaning of our experience. Help our won't learners adjust. Give them choices.

Just as consumers comparison shop for everything from the lowest interest rates to the best long-distance plans, it should come as no surprise that many parents are shopping around for the best-fit schools for their children. They no longer have to look only to the private sector for choice. Charter schools, alternative schools, magnet schools, and open enrollment policies are giving parents choices among schools while staying within the public school system. A neighborhood school is not the only public option anymore. Parents now have more information about school performance and can pick accordingly. Also, research showing that children have different learning styles has prompted some parents to look beyond neighborhood schools to find the best fit for their child. "Parents' radar is up. They are asking a lot of questions," says Jeanne Allen, president of the Center for Educational Reform in Washington, D.C. "Choice has become an answer to a lot of concerns" (Black 1998). Choice is the answer for our won't learners.

Open enrollment offers one option for parents. They can exercise choice by simply selecting which public school they wish their children to attend through open enrollment policies, which vary widely by state. Another option in the public sector is magnet schools, which offer focused curriculum in areas such as science or the performing arts. In 2000, there were 4,000 magnet schools across the country, mostly in urban areas.

Charter schools and alternative schools are the hottest development in the public choice movement. Some of these schools focus on a specialized curriculum (Native Arts High School, Hmong Culture Elementary, or New Visions with its brain-based reading program, for example). Others are designed for students at risk of dropping out. Some emphasize a back-to-basics style of teaching with uniform requirements and character education.

These schools outline a mission and establish performance goals in their "charter," which is a contract between the school and the sponsoring agency that must be met if the school is to stay open.

The appeal of alternative schools and charter schools is that they are personalized and student centered. In 2000, about 519,000 students attended charter schools alone (one percent of public school students nationwide). This is up 20 percent from 1999.

Charter schools and alternative schools call for high expectations, something that appeals to the won't learners. At many alternative schools, there are no classrooms and no bells ringing in a traditional sense. Yet students are learning. One key difference between these schools and traditional schools is the emphasis on project-based learning. The students learn by doing. Projects are completed to meet state and district requirements for math, science, and communications as well as for English and social studies.

The staff and administration are more concerned with creating an independent learner rather than a student who just regurgitates information. The students feel a sense of ownership and there are few discipline problems. We are seeing amazing results. What is even more amazing is that the students have often been referred by their home schools because of a lack of attendance, a lack of credits, or at risk of dropping out. These same students are attending school daily, making up credits, and achieving success.

With an average enrollment of about 250 to 300 students, charter and alternative schools are generally smaller than traditional public schools.

As a result of smaller class size, students receive more one-on-one help. A sense of community often emerges as parents get involved.

For example, Mario's two children were overwhelmed in a large school in his Los Angeles neighborhood. Now he drives his second and fifth grader five miles into economically challenged South Central Los Angeles for what he feels is a better education at the Accelerated Alternative School. In many cities, students will often choose to ride city buses forty-five minutes to an hour from homes in various parts of their cities to a school of their choice. Compared to class sizes of thirty to thirty-five at their neighborhood schools, these choice schools have a ratio of fifteen students to one teacher. Many have volunteers who assist in the classroom. Parents also spend time helping with reading and mathematics. "There is a warm camaraderie among the students. They all take care of each other," one parent said.

It has been stated many times recently that we need schools that are innovative and accountable. Ultimately, it's up to parents to check out the performance of competing schools. Look closely at your child's interests. What environment works best for him or her? Visit schools. Sit in the classrooms. Ask administrators to review curricula, grade reports, and teacher qualifications.

Alternative environments for students have become one of the fastest growing educational reforms of the new century. Depending on your perspective, alternative school environments may represent the most fundamental change in public education since the introduction of computers, the initiation of special education classes, and *Brown vs. the Board of Education*. We need schools that will declare what they will do for students and then provide solid evidence to families and to taxpayers that they are doing what they promised.

Governments, businesses, and schools are being shaken by change. The needs of those we serve are changing and many of our established practices no longer work. Organizations are responding in different ways. Many have crumbled; others notice nothing. Still others are thinking and behaving in dramatic new ways based on the application of sound learning principles of organized design. Society is becoming more and more involved in thinking about and planning for tomorrow's world. The increasing numbers of poor and minority children, many who are won't learners, is creating a new and formidable set of tasks for the country and its educators. The reality is that alongside the poverty and the unemployment, the street fights, and the drug deals, we can find a wealth of cultural, economic, educational, and social resources. We need only look around us.

We cannot teach our won't learners or instill in them any sense of hope or accomplishment if they are not in school. We must encourage the development and creation of schools that empower students to be lifelong learners who are self-directed and to be politically active citizens able to participate and prosper in their communities.

Alternative environments are no panacea. They must carry out their missions and goals, day to day. As one teacher, after more than thirty years in the traditional system, said, "I love this, it's the most exciting position I've ever had. It's hard, but I'm having fun." These hard jobs are producing results for the won't learners.

Frederick Douglass, the eloquent spokesperson for the antislavery movement, said, "If there is no struggle, there is no progress." Persistence is critical. We are creating schools that are having a significant, positive impact on the achievement of students, especially the won't learners. These schools are reaching out to parents, use more numerous active learning techniques, and are helping families understand how they can promote their children's learning. These schools also validate and acknowledge the traditions of culturally diverse students, help students develop a realistic and positive self-concept, and provide the literacy skills (accessing, thinking, and communicating) necessary for survival in the twenty-first century. Education is changing as well, undergoing reform in order to prepare our learners to lead productive lives in this new millennium.

Business leaders comment that their companies need entrepreneurial minds and intellectual capital. People who can think, read, write, and add. What is wrong with teaching people how to think? Corporations need people who can think and be willing to put their knowledge to the test.

We must ask ourselves: Would issues for the won't learners disappear if schools focused on strengthening core curricula, setting high expectations, improving discipline, and forgetting about retrying failed ideas?

The world is open-ended. We don't know what we will learn tomorrow. Consider the old adage: life can only be understood backwards, but life must be lived forward. The won't learners relate to this. And remember, not all children need, or want, to learn Latin or French, take math for twelve years, or read from a "Great Books" list that, at best, has been randomly compiled. Instead, they should be free to pursue the things that are of interest and at which they are adroit. If that were allowed, education would no longer be viewed by the won't learners as tortuous and mind numbing. Learning would be exciting and productive.

Welcome criticism and change. Constructive criticism is the lifeblood of healthy schools, just as it is the keynote of democracy. With it, conditions may be improved; without it, progress may never occur. The dialogue begins but does not end. The discourses that disrupt are powerful.

Welcome competition. History has proven, time and time again, that where competition does not exist, mediocrity ensues. Nowhere is this truer than in many of America's public schools.

It is also widely accepted that the cultures of schools have a direct bearing on students' learning. Schools that get results are places where adults work hard, focus on improvement, feel good about their work and themselves, and believe that they make a difference in the lives of their students.

The time has come for American education to move on toward solutions that will benefit all learners and their families. Education can only improve when schools become learning organizations not only for students but also for teachers, parents, and community stakeholders. What better way to capture the minds of the won't learners than to enroll them in schools they want to attend and that are tailored to their individual interests and needs.

Where do we go from here? The won't learners and their parents need choices.

- Specialty schools. (Examples are Boston Latin School, founded in 1635, or New York's Brooklyn Technical High School.) Admission standards are high and they are enrolling only the top achievers. For example, in 1991, New York City's three academically selective high schools had more than 40,000 applicants. Only the highest 5,500 could be accommodated.
- Magnet schools. A distinctive curriculum or instructional approach is provided. These schools draw students from beyond an assigned

attendance zone. The theme is sharply defined (a computer magnet, American Indian magnet, aviation magnet, etc.).

- Alternative schools. These schools are distinct with regard to organizational issues. Whereas the emphasis of magnet schools typically
lies in their curricular themes, alternative schools are likely to have
a broader programmatic focus, which extends beyond traditional
matters of curriculum and instructional method. The building itself
may not look like a school. There are trips and retreats, with focus
on human relations and democratic governance.

- Charter schools. This new wave of schools was created in the 1990s
by parents and teachers to meet the needs of individual students.
The students are engaged in creative, innovative, authentic learning. Course content is often tied closely to the needs of the students, and efforts are made to make courses more engaging and
relevant. Greater emphasis is placed on hands-on and experiential
learning; students are given greater responsibility for their own
success.

Despite the current discourse that vouchers or for-profit, private, and
charter schools will save education in the United States, the real work of
achieving excellence for our won't learners and for all students will most
likely occur in the nation's free and accessible public schools. Policymakers, educators, and parents are asking that all students meet high
standards. To achieve this goal, we must convert our educational system
from a filter that screens some children out to a pump that propels all
children forward.

Every day, our public schools welcome students, regardless of their
language, family circumstances, income, religious belief, nationality, citizenship, physical or mental disability, sexual orientation, race, or ethnic
origin. The inclusive nature of public education makes the work a special challenge, but not an impossible one.

No one educational program can meet the needs of all children. Public school personnel, parents, and community members must address
the different ways that children learn and how public school systems can
provide the best education for all learners. Learning is about making
connections between subjects, across disciplines, over time, and from
individual to universal experiences.

What makes a good school? What type of school will address the needs of our won't learners? There are no stock answers, but there are some universal truths. A good school is a community of parents, teachers, and students. A good school, like a good class, is run by someone with a vision who has passion and compassion. A good school has teachers who still enjoy the challenge, no matter what their age or experience. A good school prepares its students not just for the SATs or ACTs but also for the world around them.

Good schools are able to have freedom and resources to test bold new ideas, allowing good things to happen. The health of the school rests on the values, behaviors, and attitudes of its members. Tolerance, respect, and a willingness to learn from each other are critical. Democratic nations thrive on these values; they are the values we must practice and teach. Students need to know that we are there to find out more about them, to hear who they are and what they care about. The simple act of asking students has power. The convention itself ignites motivation. Listening to and learning from our won't learners as they speak out on a variety of viewpoints and a range of issues to change their world is critical to educational reform.

"Kids want to see the relevance of what they are learning," says Superintendent Sue Cleveland of Rio Rancho, New Mexico. "They want real-life experience." She goes on to say that students learn better when instruction builds on what they already know, teaches them how to express ideas, and develops activities on the basis of student interest.

We must learn to value nonconformists. We must allow a classroom atmosphere in which everyone—students and teachers—can speak their minds. Point the way toward a practical future. This isn't just about what a student wants to be when he or she grows up, it's about what is required to get there. Neither a teacher nor a staff member has the right to determine the fate of the learner, nor to determine whether he or she is going to work at McDonald's. If he or she chooses to, fine, but the student must be given the tools to become whatever he or she wants to become. Therefore, the curriculum must be shaped not only from what adults know but also from how kids learn and what they are interested in.

Good schools offer personalized learning. There is a personal relationship between teacher and child. Respect the unique way a child perceives the world and shape the way a child is going to learn accordingly. Respect the learner as a person who is connected to a family, the community, and the larger things in life.

A good school is a place where students like to be. Joy, a sense of thrill and satisfaction, should accompany work. Unfunny places collect casualties. A school with humor thrives.

In crafting a school's culture, the staff and administrators are models, potters, poets, actors, and healers. They are historians and anthropologists. They are visionaries and dreamers. Our won't learners thrive in a positive culture where staff have a shared sense of purpose, where they pour their hearts into teaching. Our won't learners thrive in an environment where the underlying norms are of collegiality, improvement, and hard work. They thrive when rituals and traditions celebrate student accomplishment, teacher innovation, and parental commitment. They especially thrive when success, joy, and humor abound.

Without supportive, student-centered cultures, reforms will falter, staff morale and commitment will wither, and student learning will slip. School leaders shape the culture by communicating core values in what they say and do. Honor and recognize those who have worked to serve students. Observe rituals and traditions to support the heart and soul of the school. Eloquently speak of the deeper mission of the school. Create an inviting exterior and cheerful, warm interior that set the tone for an environment in which parents, students, and community members feel welcome and wanted.

The ultimate goal of our efforts is to promote the *common good*. Schools must serve society and meet the needs of individual students and their families. Schools serve the larger society in multiple ways—by preparing active citizens who are vital to a robust democracy; by preparing knowledgeable workers who are essential for a thriving economy; by encouraging students to be caring and compassionate people who will seek a more just society; and by preparing lifelong learners who will continue to use education as a means to improve the quality of life for themselves and others.

Difficulty in educating our won't learners remains an ongoing problem. Attendance in the traditional public schools is low, academic achievement is below average and the dropout rate remains high. However, in recent years, communication has somewhat helped bridge the gap between traditional and alternative education. Won't learners are unique individuals and their culture and environmental background is what makes him or her unique. Alternative school systems have emerged to help foster this uniqueness. Reform and systematic restructuring is happening.

Interviews show that parents do not believe the traditional public school system is capable of teaching their won't learners, many of whom are non-Caucasian. They advocate for schools that are cutting edge, innovative, and experimental. When their children attend these schools, they see improved performance. Academic grades are better than at previous schools, attendance has skyrocketed, and attitude and behavior toward learning have shown significant gains. Fewer students are dropping out. When the media says that parents of non-Caucasians should "work for change within the system," the parents interviewed retort that the history of working within the system has not been a good one. Many parents believe charter schools and alternative schools are affecting our won't learners in a positive manner.

New and innovative alternative programs will have an impact on existing public schools and their won't learners. These schools and their programs offer what parents want:

- Parents want to be integral members of the educational team. The parents interviewed have a deep commitment to participating in their child's education.
- Parents want curriculum that promotes cultural competence and appreciates ethnic diversity (teaching the history, language, stories, and values of the culture).
- Parents want instructional methods that promote cooperation, interaction, and success for their children. This includes the use of culturally resonant strategies, examples, and analogies.
- Parents want assessment practices that include alternative methods, which will allow for cultural differences and encourage community review to ensure an equitable approval of student's work.
- Parents want a school culture of oneness that supports student growth.
- Parents want classrooms that do not conflict with the values of the community.
- Parents want school programs that ensure a quality education for children of poverty. (Past and present conditions of racism contribute to reduced expectations, opportunities, and resources for children who live in poverty.)
- Parents want accountability where they see clear-cut goals, leading to improved academic performance.

To achieve success, our won't learners must be given the opportunity to attend a school where they are assured of:

- Teachers and administrators who provide the extra support system necessary for improved performance
- A learning environment that is safe
- Achieving at the highest level
- Being accepted as individuals
- Learning is collaboration, not isolation
- Applying what is learned to cultural projects, activities, community service, and real-world situations
- Receiving the skills needed to meet the demands of a changing society, with core essentials of the basics (reading, writing, mathematics, and reasoning) allowing them to become involved citizens and contributors to the community.

The teachers who work with our won't learners begin where the students are, not on the first page of a curriculum guide. These teachers accept and build upon the premise that learners differ in important ways (interests, backgrounds, learning styles). They are ready to engage students in instruction through different learning modalities, by appealing to different interests and by using varied rates of instruction along with varied degrees of complexity.

In alternative schools, we find teachers providing specific ways for each individual to learn as deeply as possible and as quickly as possible, without assuming one student's roadmap for learning is identical to anyone else's. Students are held to high standards and come to believe that learning involves effort, risk, and personal triumph.

Teachers working with our won't learners appear to use time flexibly, call upon a range of instructional strategies, and become partners with their students to shape the learning environment. They do not force-fit learners into a standard mold. You might say the teachers are students of their students.

The teachers are more in touch with their students. They unconditionally accept the students as they are and expect them to become all that they can be. In other words, the teachers accept, embrace, and plan for the fact that learners may bring many commonalties to school, but that learners also bring essential differences that make them individuals.

The teachers interviewed all embraced the following five beliefs:

- Won't learners want to change inside but find it difficult to do so unless things outside are changed as well. The simplistic solution of "more education" is meaningless when a society is not tuned in to academic achievement.
- Respect the readiness level of each student.
- Expect all learners to grow and then support their continued growth.
- Offer all students the opportunity to explore essential understandings and skills at degrees of difficulty that escalate consistently as they develop their understanding and skill.
- Offer students assignments and tasks that look and are equally interesting, equally important, and equally engaging.

We cannot move forward unless we look at learning styles. Differences in learning styles requires an adjustment in how all students are taught, not just our won't learners. Schools need to individualize a program for each student. We must develop innovative programs that meet the needs of the population we serve. By building on what students come with and know and by determining their learning styles, alternative school programs can expand the knowledge and skills of the students they serve.

We think, learn, and create in different ways. The development of our potential is affected by the match between what we learn and how we learn, using our particular experiences as the foundation.

Despite compelling new educational knowledge, traditional public schools have changed little over the past one hundred years. The assumption remains that a child of a given age is enough like all other children of the same age that he or she should traverse the same curriculum in the same fashion with all other students of that age. Further, schools continue to act as though all children need to finish classroom tasks as near to the same moment as possible.

Howard Gardner contributed greatly to the awareness that students vary in intelligence, preferences, or strengths. While Gardner is clear that intelligences are interrelated, he is also convinced that there are important differences among them. Teachers working with our won't learners facilitate the learning process by attending to these differences when planning and carrying out instruction. Teaching is targeted to the variable learning needs of diverse students.

Today's teachers still contend with the essential challenge of the one-room schoolhouse and how to reach out effectively to students who span the spectrum of learning readiness, personal interests, culturally shaped ways of seeing and speaking of the world, and the experiences in that world. The biggest mistake of past centuries in teaching has been to treat all children as if they were variants of the same individual, and thus feel justified in teaching them the same subjects in the same way. Alternative educational programs feel right to our won't learners who learn in a multitude of different ways, at different rates, and these learners also bring to school different talents and interests.

Schools that give their learners a solid foundation in their personal and cultural identity are encouraging academic improvement. Teaching about and from the cultures of all students is more than a political statement; it is sound educational theory. Students construct knowledge by incorporating new understanding with the knowledge they bring into the classroom.

Stephen Covey says, "To begin with the end in mind means to start with a clear understanding of your destination. It means to know where you are going so that you better understand where you are now so that the steps you take are always in the right direction."

Once the won't learner begins to see the end and understand his or her destination, learning starts to take place. Education becomes a driving force.

During the past two decades, more and more students, especially those from poor socioeconomic backgrounds, have felt a catastrophic decline in the ability of their environment to provide adequate resources, support, and opportunities that are fundamental for growth and development into positive adulthood. Look at the statistics. As we ended the twentieth century, an American child was:

- Killed by guns every two hours
- Arrested for a violent crime every five minutes
- Born to a teenaged mother every fifty-nine seconds
- Born into poverty every thirty seconds
- Born to an unmarried mother every twenty-six seconds
- Abused or neglected every thirteen seconds (Data provided by Meyer and Bauers-Northrup.)

Alternative systems have entered the arena of school reform to act as a catalyst for improvement throughout the public school system and society in general. A high proportion of won't learners can be termed "square-peg" kids who do not fit the round holes of conventional schools. Alternative systems prepare these students to become whole, well-rounded young people who can interact with the world around them. Parents see these new programs as a solution to poor test scores, dropout rates, truancy, and behavior issues. The emphasis is on the individual. The student is taught in a way that maximizes his or her potential.

Public schools were created on the premise that education would be the great social equalizer. Yet due to inertia or tradition, too few schools are preparing students to compete in the Information Age. Change is the most talked about and the least acted-upon concept in the school reform movement. If bringing about change means injecting a productive level of stress and tension within traditional public schools, so be it. We need to loosen the grip that stifles creativity and risk-taking.

Albert Einstein once remarked, "We cannot solve a problem with the same thinking we used to create it." The time has come for society to reappraise the way it educates children. The public school system, despite occasional lip service to the idea of individuality, has really been at war with individuality. It is the denial of individuality, the idea that everyone must follow some general plan, that is at the core of the failure of many schools. It is time to create an environment in which schools not only operate effectively but also recognize and respond to the fact that all learners are different and have different needs. It is time to create an environment that nurtures and encourages individuality instead of treating it as irrelevant.

Powerful forces are creating fundamental changes in social, economical, political, and educational systems in our highly interdependent world. To succeed in this changing world, schools must be based on values, focused on mission, centered on relationships, and oriented toward the future. Engaging with others within and outside education is essential for creating the synergy necessary to achieve our purpose. We must also be flexible, participatory, and externally attuned to foster reciprocal relationships and self-renewal.

When working with our won't learners, schools need a vision. Clear goals are established, and administration, faculty, and students work together to meet those goals. The teachers are empowered. They know their voices count, whether dealing with students or initiating changes in curriculum. The kids feel empowered, too. There is an atmosphere where it is "cool" to be smart and to learn. The students begin to discover that success in school is one way to improve their lives.

Our won't learners know the meaning of success and how to succeed. "This is me, Dr. D.," said one young woman, and she read the following quote:

> To laugh often and love much, to win the respect of intelligent persons and the affection of children; to earn the approbation of honest citizens and endure the betrayal of false friends; to appreciate beauty; to find the best in others; to give one's self; to leave the world a little better; whether by a healthy child, a garden patch, or a redeemed social condition; to have played and laughed with enthusiasm and seeing with exultation; to know even one life has breathed easier because you have lived—this is to have succeeded.

She had just discovered Ralph Waldo Emerson and had the insight to relate this passage to her life. Like this young woman, our won't learners can learn and want to learn. There must be a strong school support system in place to help make this happen.

The walls are coming down between the disciplines, between faculty and parents, between students and the teachers, and between the school and the community. We need to break the traditional mold of students confined to experiences within the school building and teachers isolated in their classrooms. Students must be encouraged to spend part of their day in a community business or with a mentor. The students can work with a group of elementary school youngsters, visit the elderly at a nursing home or senior citizen high-rise, conduct on-site research, or take a postsecondary class at a local college. The students need to be connected with the community beyond the classroom door. In short, schools need to supplement the diminishing influence of family, neighborhood, and church in order to offer their students a life experience, not just a school experience.

In the absence of ideal conditions and in our imperfect society, many schools are proof that the entire system need not be changed in order to make vast improvements in individual schools. It's too easy to wait for the revolution that will create a wondrous new educational system. It is harder to look at existing schools and improve them in small but significant ways.

Every school can be improved by giving new support systems to students who are in trouble. A faculty or peer mentor for a student who is experiencing difficulty can change the entire school environment by cutting into undercurrents of anger and anti-intellectualism.

Our children deserve a world-class education. We need to demand an end to public schools that provide a one-size-fits-all education. Let's move to a more open, democratic system that provides real choices to meet diverse student interests. Let's have a legacy of high standards, high expectations for student performance and offer abundant options to students and their families.

It has become clear that each student will choose, of his or her own free will, the direction of his or her life. The power of the human will, the free will, cannot be ignored in the education equation. To educate our won't learners means that we must recognize and accept the truth that all the education in the world is for naught unless the student chooses, of his or her own free will, to accept that education.

We educators do not, nor can we, control our students' wills. We are at best equal partners in the educational process. If we hope to guide our students toward a positive life, we must continue to be role models for them. If we hope to inspire, encourage, and challenge our students to make life-giving decisions and make choices of their own free wills, we must be forming relationships with them. We must walk beside them, talk to them, and share our lives with them.

I entered the field of public education in 1965, hoping to make a difference in the lives of the least advantaged, to educate them for economic prosperity. Thirty-some years later, I created an alternative school, still hoping to make a difference in the lives of the least advantaged. I know, from my own experience, that such schools can truly make a difference in the lives of our young citizens.

Peter Palmer (1993) states that, "Education is the slave of an economic system that wants to master and manipulate nature, society and even the human heart in order to gain profit and power." Within such an economic system, every relationship becomes an I-It. In reality, education requires I-You relationships. Such relationships spring from the response of a free will to a profound sense of belonging. As we reinvent education for this new century, we need schools that are structured for community and caring, and for developing I-You relationships.

In his book *Land Thou*, Martin Buber (1970) speaks of I-It and I-You relationships. When we choose our friends for the purposes of utility of pleasure, we create an I-It relationship. The I-You wishes well to the other for his or her own sake. I-You forms partnerships based on equality, giving choices, inspiring free will, and sharing.

There are no quick fixes for the problems that plague public education. If we hope to create schools that are positive learning communities, schools that inspire students to make positive decisions and choices of their own free will, it will require our total commitment. The work may be exhausting but the reward will be a school that is an ideal place for students, parents, teachers, and community members.

The public educational system in the United States has served this nation well. Today and in the future, this system will meet unprecedented challenges. The time is right to assess its strengths and weaknesses. We must trust that our won't learners can succeed.

Only in America, a musical message by Brooks and Dunn, speaks to us all:

> Sun coming up over New York City
> School bus driver in a traffic jam
> Staring at the faces in her rearview mirror
> Looking at the promise of the Promised Land
> One kid dreams of fame and fortune
> One kid helps to pay the rent
> One could end up going to prison
> One just might be president.
> We all get a chance
> Everybody gets to dance
> Only in America
> Dreaming in red, white, and blue,
> Only in America
> Dream big as we want to.

Ask yourselves how far you are willing to go to help our won't learners. We *must* encourage them to hope, to dream, and to dance.

BIBLIOGRAPHY

INTRODUCTION

Bushweller, K. 1999. A generation of cheaters. *The American School Board Journal* 186, no. 4 (April): 24–32.

Hirschberg, L. 1999. Teenseltown. *New York Times Magazine* (5 September): 42–49, 74–79.

Males, M. 1996. *The scapegoat generation: America's war on adolescents*. Monroe, Me.: Common Courage Press.

Nathan, J. 1996. *Charter schools*. San Francisco, Calif.: Jossey-Bass.

Public Agenda. 1999. *Kids these days, 99: What Americans really think about the next generation*. Washington, D.C.: U.S. Department of Education Press.

CHAPTER 1

American Institute for Research. 1999. *Looking to the future*. Washington, D.C.: American Institute for Research.

Cicchelli, T., and S. Marcus. 1995. Three high school alternative schooling models: A response to at-risk learners. *NASSP Curriculum Report* 24: 1–4.

Dewey, J. 1916. *Democracy and education*. New York: Random House.

DeYoung, C. 1995. *Coming together*. Valley Forge, Penn.: Judson Press.

Hatch, T. 1998. How comprehensive can comprehensive reform be? *Phi Delta Kappan* 79, no. 7: 518–22.

Kozol, J. 1991. *Savage inequalities: Children in America's schools*. New York: Harper.

Nathan, J. 1996. *Charter schools*. San Francisco, Calif.: Jossey-Bass.

———. 2000. Quoted by Greve, K. in Look, Jane, Look: Charter schools push the educational envelope. *Minnesota Monthly* 34, no. 9: 52–53, 142–45.

Ravitch, D. 2000. *Left back: A century of failed school reforms*. New York: Simon & Schuster.

Takaki, R. 1999. A different mirror: A conversation with Ronald Takaki. *Education Leadership* 56, no. 7: 8–13.

U.S. Department of Education. 1997. *A study of charter schools: First year report*. Washington, D.C.: Office of Education Research and Improvement.

———. 1998. *Profiles of successful schoolwide programs*. Washington, D.C.: Author.

CHAPTER 2

Friedman, M. 1962. *Capitalism and freedom*. Chicago, Ill.: Chicago University Press.

Harrington, M. 1962. *The other America*. New York: Macmillan.

Kozol, J. 1991. *Savage inequalities: Children in America's schools*. New York: Harper.

New York City Public Schools, 1998–1999. 2000. *OER Report*. Brooklyn, N.Y.: New York City Board of Education, Office of Educational Research.

Olson, L., and C. Jerald. 1998. Barriers to success. *Education Week* 42, no. 17: 9.

U.S. Census Bureau. 1999. *Income and poverty*. Washington, D.C.: U.S. Dept. of Commerce.

CHAPTER 3

Dewey, J. 1916. *Democracy and education*. New York: Random House.

Traina, R. 1999. What makes a teacher good? *Education Week* 18, no. 19 (20 January): 34.

U.S. Department of Health, Education, and Welfare. 1966. *Equality of educational opportunity: Summary report* (The Coleman Report). Washington, D.C.: Government Printing Office.

CHAPTER 4

Galinsky, E. 1999. *Ask the children*. New York: William Morrow.
Lindle, J. 1989. What do parents want from principals and teachers? *Educational Leadership* 47, no. 2: 12–14.
Norton, K. 2000. Testimony before the Subcommittee on Oversight and Investigations Committee on Education and Workforce. Bloomington, Minn. 6 June.
Public Agenda Report. 2000. Washington, D.C.: Office of Educational Research.
U.S. Census Bureau. 2000. *Families, 2000.* Washington, D.C.: U.S. Census Bureau Printing Office.

CHAPTER 5

Braddock, B., and C. McPartland. 1998. *Authentic teaching and learning for all students.* New York: Free Press.
Gardner, H. 1983. *Frames of mind: A theory of multiple intelligences.* New York: Basic Books.
———. 1991. *The unschooled mind: How children think and how schools should teach.* New York: Basic Books.
Langdon, P. 2000. Big vs. small. *The American Enterprise* (January): 21–23.
Maeroff, G. 1998. Making it better for school children in need. *Phi Delta Kappan* 79, no. 6: 425–32.
Meier, D. 1995. *The power of their ideas.* Boston, Mass.: Beacon Press.
———. 2000. Smaller is better. *The Nation* (5 June): 8–15.
Mitchell, S. 2000. Small schools foster big gains in learning. *The Progressive Populist* (1 October): 13–17.
U.S. National Commission on Literacy. 1997. *A study and first year report.* Washington, D.C.: Office of Educational Research and Improvement.

CHAPTER 6

Apple, M. 1990. *Ideology and curriculum.* New York: Routledge.
Commission of Education and America's Future Report. 1997. Washington, D.C.: U.S. Dept. of Education Press.
Cotton, K. 1996. *School size, school climate, and student performance.* School Improvement Research Series, Close-up # 20. Portland, Ore.: Northwestern Regional Laboratory.

Darling-Hammond, L. 1997. *Doing what matters most: Investing in quality teaching*. New York: National Commission on Teaching and America's Future.

National Center on Child Abuse and Neglect. 1999. *National child abuse and neglect data system* (May). Working paper no. 2. Washington, D.C.: U.S. Department of Health and Human Services.

National Staff Development Council. 1998. *Standards for staff development*. Oxford, Ohio: Basic Books.

Peter D. Hart Research Associates. 1999. *Survey: The New Face of Retirement*.

Raywid, M. 1997/1998. Small schools: A reform that works. *Educational Leadership* 55, no. 4 (December/January): 34–39.

Schmoker, M. 1996. *Results: The key to continuous school improvement*. Alexandria, Va.: ASCD.

U.S. Census Bureau. 1999. *Poverty in the United States*. Washington, D.C.: United States Department of Commerce, table 17.

———. 2000. Who's minding the kids? Childcare arrangements (October) <www.census.gov/prod/2000pubs/p70-70.pdf>.

Wasley, R., M. Fine, M. Gladden, N. Holland, S. King, E. Mosak, and L. Powell. 2000. Small schools: Great strides—a study of new small schools in Chicago. New York: Bank Street College of Education. www.bankstreet.edu/html/news/smallschools.pdf>.

CHAPTER 7

Clark, J. 1999. Growing high school reform: Planting the seeds of systemic change. *NASSP Bulletin* 83, no. 606: 1–9.

Urban Learners. 2000. *St. Paul Pioneer Press*, 18 June.

CHAPTER 8

Black, S. 1998. Research: Parent support. *The American School Board Journal* 185, no. 4: 50–54.

Buber, M. 1970 (1923). *Land thou*. Trans., W. Kaufmann. New York: Charles Scribner's.

Covey, S. 2000. *Seven habits of highly effective people*. New York: Running Press.

Gardner, H. 1983. *Frames of mind: A theory of multiple intelligences*. New York: Basic Books.

Massey, J. 1985. *Spiritual disciplines*. Grand Rapids, Mich.: Francis Asbury Press.

Meyer, A., and W. Bauers-Northrup. 1997. What is prevention anyway? *Educational Leadership* 54, no. 8: 31–35.

New York Public Schools, 1992–1993. 1994. *OER Report*. Brooklyn, N.Y.: New York City Board of Education, Office of Educational Research.

Palmer, P. 1993. *To know as we are known: Education as a spiritual journey*. San Francisco, Calif.: Harper.

Ravitch, D., and J. Viteritti. 1997. *New schools for a new century*. New Haven, Conn.: Yale University Press.

ABOUT THE AUTHOR

Dr. Darlene Leiding, principal (K–12) and director of special education at Heart of the Earth Center for Indian Education Charter School, has been involved in the field of education for over thirty-five years. She is involved in the charter school movement and is also a recognized expert in the realm of alternative educational programs. Dr. Leiding created Volunteers of America Alternative Elementary School and Volunteers of America Alternative High School and was their director of schools for three years.

Dr. Leiding received her doctorate in educational leadership from the University of St. Thomas in St. Paul, Minnesota, in 1999, with special emphasis on the reasons American Indian students improve their academics when enrolled in alternative programs or charter schools. Dr. Leiding's most recent research into the learning styles of inner-city youth brought her face to face with the question: "What can educators do to reconnect with today's youth, many of whom are won't learners."